Don't Put Out the Burning Bush

edited by

Vivian Boland OP

Don't Put Out the Burning Bush:

Worship and Preaching in a Complex World

edited by

Vivian Boland OP

ATF Press
Adelaide

Cover design by Astrid Sengkey

ATF Press
An imprint of the Australasian Theological Forum Ltd
P O Box 504
Hindmarsh
SA 5007
ABN 90 116 359 963
www.atfpress.com

Contents

Introduction

'Gestis verbisque': Proclaiming the Mystery of Christ in Action and Words

Vivian Boland OP

Word and ritual, sign and symbol

The chapters that follow consider questions about preaching and liturgy, in particular the relationship between them. Because the authors belong to different Christian denominations (but not only for that reason) the reader will detect certain complementary anxieties, on the one hand that preaching is in danger of being overshadowed by liturgy and on the other that liturgy is in danger of being overshadowed by preaching. For theological and other reasons, might it not be the case that liturgy (ritual, sacramental worship) will get in the way of, and even take away from, preaching? Is not the preaching of the gospel itself the 'rational worship', *logike latreia,* to which Saint Paul calls the Christians of Rome (Rom 12:1, and see Jn 4:23)? On the other hand, for theological and for other reasons, might it not be the case that preaching (the heaping up of human words, the commentary that accompanies liturgical actions) will get in the way of, and even take away from, the inherent power of the liturgical, ritual, sacramental action itself? Is not the doing of this action in remembrance of Him the central act of worship to which Saint Paul calls the Christians of Corinth (1 Cor 11:23–26) on the basis of a tradition he had received, going back to Jesus himself (1 Cor 11:23; Matt 26:26–29; Mk 14:22–25; Lk 22:14–20)?

An initial response to these anxieties is to wonder where the suggestion comes from in the first place that word and ritual should be at odds with each other rather than supporting each other. (Let us leave aside for the moment the fact that most of us will have had experiences that support *both* anxieties.) Human language, in the normal sense of using words, is just the most privileged symbolic system that we use, the most versatile and sophisticated system of signs human beings have devised. Other symbols, and those processes of sign-making that we call rituals, are always also used in human communication, even within those forms of it that seem purely verbal. There is an order to be followed, conventions of grammar to be observed, and protocols to be respected if the sounds that come from our throats or the words that appear on our screens are to do what language is meant to do: establish communion between a speaker and a hearer (or a writer and a reader) in order to communicate meaning and truth, to define and identify, and to bind both parties in some shared life, however superficial or transitory. There cannot be language, words bearing meaning, without supporting signs, symbols and rituals.

Likewise the use of bodily gestures, physical things or human artifacts in symbolic or ritual actions, while itself a form of communication, cannot be so effectively without the use of words. Sooner or later someone is bound to ask 'what does it mean?', or 'what are you doing?', perhaps even 'what are we doing?' The poet, artist or musician might immediately warn us of the danger of looking beyond the artifact or action for an explanatory meaning that would deny the aesthetic or symbolic power of the poem, or painting, or music. 'If I could have said it in words, I would have said it in words', we sometimes hear them saying.

We must heed their warning while expressing one of our own. There is a kind of rationalism or intellectualism that can regard the use of symbol and ritual as somehow 'irrational', addressed to levels of human experience that are not susceptible to being thought about and spoken about in ordinary human words. This may then be endorsed by romanticist views or psychological concerns that seem content with such a separation. One cones-quence of setting up an opposition between 'rational word' and 'irrational symbol' (even if it is then to be 'rationalised' into words) is that identified by Mary Douglas:

> One of the gravest problems of our day is the lack of commitment to common symbols. If this were all, there would be little to say. If it were merely a matter of our fragmentation into small groups, each committed to its proper symbolic forms, the case would be simple to understand. But more mysterious is a wide-spread, explicit rejection of rituals as such. Ritual is become a bad word signifying empty conformity (*Natural Symbols*, London, 1973, 19).

More recently, Rowan Williams has written that there is

> . . . little enough symbolic therapy (if I may coin a term) in our societies to reinforce a sense of common need or dependence, and a contingency and vulnerability we share as finite agents. All the more important, then, to resist anything that trivializes or shrinks the symbolic range of our sacramental practice (*On Christian Theology*, Blackwells, 2000, 221).

A response to such diagnoses, frequently proposed and pursued in the time since Douglas wrote, will stress the importance of ritual and symbol in human experience but in a way that continues to regard them as merely illustrative of what could still be fully (and perhaps more effectively) stated in words alone. There can be a paternalistic, even elitist, aspect to this (and this goes back to the origins of philosophy itself), that those who can will understand and use the word (*logos*) while those who for some reason can not will be happy with the use of myth (*muthos*), with its accompanying symbols and rituals. (Another way of putting this is to say that those who can, will seek to know, while those who can not, will be content with faith.) But ritual then seems contrived, a kind of visual aid for the less educated or the emotionally needy, and it is not surprising that many people would begin to think of it as 'empty ritual'. The flip side is that even in such efforts to defend ritual, human communication is still being 'spiritualised' and disembodied, soul and body circling round one another as it were but without integration, without harmony, and so not fully human. (Rowan Williams' comment quoted above is not entirely free from this danger.)

Our next, 'theological', move is not to say that because full human communication is like this, needing word and symbolic action, so God's revelation comes to us in this way (although this way of putting it is not untrue). Rather the next thing to say is that 'the Word became flesh' and so we see more clearly what fully human communication and communion involve. It is not that we know what 'word' and 'sign' are to mean and then shape our understanding of Christ around that. For Anthony Kenny the understanding of sign is one of the questions that theology clarified for philosophy and not vice versa (*A Brief History of Western Philosophy*, Blackwells, 1998, 101–04). The effort to understand the revelation that comes in Christ, the mystery of the Word and Sign that he is, and how his grace and life continue to reach us, illuminate the philosophical questions for us.

Two great witnesses speak of how this works from the point of view of what humans need and how they function. Thomas Aquinas puts it like this:

> Human beings can only arrive at intelligible and spiritual realities through physical and sensible ones. God's providence cares for each thing in accordance with its particular condition. So it is appropriate that the means whereby divine wisdom helps human beings towards salvation are the physical and sensible signs which we call 'sacraments' (*Summa theologiae* III 61,1).

Note that he is not saying that because this is our need, God must act in a particular way. God acts with supreme freedom and Aquinas is here pointing out the appropriateness (*convenientia*) of the way in which God has in fact acted. Augustine of Hippo expands on the point and (as usual) is alert to a psychological level to which Aquinas often seems indifferent:

> All these things brought home to us in figures have the aim of feeding and somehow fanning the flame of love which, like a sort of specific gravity, carries us above or within ourselves until we come to rest. Thus proposed, these realities move and enkindle love more than if they were set forth in a starkly intellectual way and not as sacraments (*sacramenta*). It is hard to say why this should be so. But it is certain that anything expressed by way of allegory

> is more moving, more pleasing and better heeded than if it were said outright in the most appropriate words. I think the soul is slower to catch fire as long as it is involved in mere earthly things; while if it is directed to bodily symbols (*similitudines*) and to the spiritual realities expressed by them in figure, this very process enlivens it, enkindles it like a waving torch and draws it with more ardent love to its resting-place (*Epistle* 55:21 [*Patrologia Latina* 33:214]).[1]

A fuller theological statement about the relationship between actions and words in the history of salvation is found in *Dei Verbum*, the Second Vatican Council's constitution on divine revelation:

> It pleased God, in his goodness and wisdom, to reveal himself and to make known the mystery of his will (*sacramentum voluntatis suae*) (cf Eph 1:9), which was that human beings might have access to the Father and become sharers in the divine nature, through Christ the Word made flesh and in the Holy Spirit (cf Eph 2:18; 2 Pet 1:4). By this revelation the invisible God (cf Col 1:15; 1 Tim 1:17), out of the richness of his love, spoke with human beings as his friends (cf Ex 33:11; Jn 15:14–15) and lived among them (cf Bar 3:(37–38), in order to

---

[1] It is interesting to note how this anticipates the distinction developed by John Henry Newman, in *A Grammar of Assent*, between *notional* and *real* assent, the one remaining intellectual and universal, the other becoming concrete and so effective.

> call them and receive them into His own company.
>
> The course of revelation is through actions and words (*gestis verbisque*) intimately bound up with each other, in such a way that the deeds (*opera*) which God performed in the history of salvation, make clear and substantiate the doctrine and the things signified by the words; and the words (*verba*) for their part proclaim the deeds of God and clarify the mystery which is at work in them. The most intimate truth of this revelation concerning God and the salvation of the human being, shines out for us in Christ, who is both mediator and fullness of revelation (cf Mt 11:27; Jn 1:14,17; 14:6; 17:1-3; 2 Cor 3:16; 4:6; Eph 1:3-14).

How revelation has been made, in the time of promise as in the time of fulfilment, is how revelation continues to be received and proclaimed, that is not just in words but also in deeds, *gestis verbisque*. The words spoken by a prophet are known to be false if what they promise does not take place (Deut 18:22) just as they are known to be true if what they promise does come about (Jer 28:9; Ezek 33:33). The love of Christians is not to be just words or mere talk but something real and active (1 Jn 3:18), not just a hearing and repeating of words but something done (James 1:22–25). The conclusion of the Sermon on the Mount brings both points together: the truth of prophecy is known from its fruits (Matt 7:15-20) and the genuine disciple is not one who repeats words, even if it is 'Lord,

Lord', but one who *acts* on the words of Jesus (Matt 7:21-27).[2]

The rituals are not simply our invention anymore than the words or moral requirements are. There must be some criterion by which to measure the faithfulness, the 'truth', of what is said and done. This criterion is Christ—that what we say and do be in continuity with the Word, the Love, the Sacrament, of God that he is. All the 'mysteries of Christ' inform not only the content but the form of our proclamation—his work of teaching and healing, his work of forgiving and community-building, his work of suffering, dying and rising from among the dead. He not only said things, he did things, and he allowed things to be done to him. The life contained and expressed in those mysteries is what we proclaim in word and deed, in preaching and teaching, in the sacramental life of the Church as in her mission of charity in the world.

Actions and words in Jesus' inauguration of the kingdom

The starting point is, then, christological rather than anthropological. The criterion is Christ, his saying and doing, his mysteries, his undergoing and being raised. As Rowan Williams puts it, 'the tradition of his deeds and words is heavily influenced by the sense that he was a sign-maker of a disturbingly revolutionary kind' (*On Christian Theology*, Blackwells, 2000, 203).

In Catholic piety the Rosary has a special place as a way of meditating on the mysteries of Christ's life, death and resurrection. It has been cherished and promoted particularly by the Order of Preachers as a method of contemplating and preaching those mysteries. John Paul

---

[2] John Henry Newman again: 'the event is the true key to prophecy', cited by Josef Pieper in *Hope and History*, Ignatius Press, San Francisco 1994, 97

II's decision to add five 'new mysteries' to the Rosary, the so-called mysteries of light, has alerted people to how strange it was before, that in meditating on the important events of the life and work of Jesus one passed from the finding in the temple (recounted in Luke 2) to the agony in the garden. Was there no significant 'mystery' between these two moments, nothing of essential spiritual, theological, revelatory or salvific importance? Thomas Aquinas says in his commentary on the Creed that all the mysteries of Christ are for our instruction, and people were encouraged to meditate on them elsewhere: healings, other miracles, parables, discourses, vocation stories, meals and other encounters, all that Jesus said and did during the time of his 'conversation' among human beings.

But picking out these five new mysteries of light—the baptism of Jesus, the wedding feast of Cana, his proclamation of the kingdom of God and call to conversion, the transfiguration, and the institution of the eucharist—gives content to the description of Jesus' public ministry as a sustained 'preaching moment': something is being communicated to people by Someone and the something that is communicated *is* the Someone who communicates it. It is, once again, a matter of deeds and words, as these five mysteries bring out, things said by Jesus the preacher and prophet, things done and undergone by Jesus the sign-maker and artist.

Jesus the preacher is anointed for his ministry at his baptism by John in the river Jordan. This marked the moment when his ministry began. An apostle, Acts 1 tells us, is one who can witness to the events from the baptism of Jesus to his resurrection. This provides the content of the Christian kerygma just as the baptism marks the moment when Jesus himself 'went public' and began to proclaim the Word of God throughout Galilee and the surrounding countryside. The theophany at the baptism is for the Baptist or for other bystanders (so Matthew), or it is for Jesus himself (so Mark and Luke), but either way the entry into his ministry involves Jesus in a clearer conviction about his vocation. It may be that one should refer here also to his temptation in the wilderness and to the moment of the Baptist's arrest. Then Jesus, in his human nature, comes to realise something about himself, that he is to be this representative figure for Israel—the servant of God, a prophet and perhaps *the* prophet, the anointed one or messiah, the son of man. The gospels recount in different ways how Jesus appropriated his vocation as a preacher and teacher, as priest, prophet and king.

As with many later moments in the public ministry of Jesus, the gospel of John gives a distinctive account of the beginning of that ministry. At the wedding feast of Cana, recounted in John 2, Jesus gave his 'first sign' and the disciples began to believe in him. His work is underway even though his hour had not yet come. Cana begins the fulfilment of Old Testament promises of the eschatological age, the banquet of fine wine, given in abundance, the out-pouring of the Spirit that is bountiful and indiscriminate, the meal offered by wisdom to her devotees (Is 25:6; Joel 3:1–5; Acts 2:13; Prov 9:1–6). But Cana also 'echoes beforehand' the moment of Jesus's death as John describes it: the hour has now come, there is blood and water flowing, there is thirst (now his own rather than that of the people around him), his mother is present and is again addressed as 'woman' (the new Eve), and there is glory, the glory first revealed in the sign of Cana, finally and definitively revealed as the glory of 'the only Son', giving his life on the cross.

The task of preaching is to bring people to see, by faith, this glory. It is a call to conversion, to turn away from sin and believe the good news of Jesus Christ, to have a new mind and be renewed, to turn away from the worship of dead things to a spiritual worship of the living God. The third 'mystery of light' is Christ's proclamation of the kingdom of God with the call to conversion. It is an invitation to enter into the mystery of Christ's ministry of preaching. Paul will explain all this at length: those who have been reconciled by Christ become ambassadors of reconciliation (2 Cor 5:20). They receive grace to announce the good news and to invite to the banquet. No particular moment in the gospel accounts of his ministry is picked out in this third mystery of light which makes it different from the other nineteen mysteries of the Rosary. It could easily have been the Sermon on the Mount, but instead people are invited to meditate on the entire teaching ministry of Jesus, all that he 'said and did' (Acts 1:1; Lk 1:1–4) in establishing the kingdom.

The glory that is being revealed yet remains hidden, and the transfiguration is often understood as a moment in which the veil of Jesus' humanity slips and a hidden divinity is revealed. But what happens in that moment is more a breaking in of the future, when the glory that is to be his, the glory of his resurrection, is glimpsed beforehand by his chosen disciples. Our preaching moments are for the most part mundane, ordinary and routine but they are always also moments of insight, illumination and revelation for someone who is listening. At least they are always these things potentially, and perhaps the one brought to fresh insight about themselves through our preaching is the one who is preaching.

If preaching were just a human message, our ideas and experiences, then we would be telling people what they know, or potentially could know, for themselves. But it is the Word that we preach, of course coming through human channels (earthen vessels at that) and so taking flesh in terms of our ideas and experiences as it takes flesh in terms of the language and accent in which we speak but with a character, depth and significance far beyond the channel through which it is communicated. As Paul says, 'we preach what Scripture calls "the things no eye has seen and no ear has heard, things beyond the mind of man, all that God has prepared for those who love him"' (1 Cor 2:9). We speak in words not taught by human wisdom (1 Cor 2:13). Where it happens that someone hears, through our preaching, what St John of the Cross calls 'the silent music of eternal love', then it is not we who speak (even though it is) but the Spirit of the heavenly Father speaking through us.

So people are taken up into a process of transfiguration, from one degree of glory to the next (2 Cor 3:18), and this is happening particularly as we partake in the daily bread of the Eucharist. The fifth mystery of light is 'the institution of the Eucharist as the sacramental expression of the paschal mystery'. This too is a strange mystery compared with all the other mysteries of the Rosary. It is not just 'the last supper', as it might have been, but 'the institution of a sacramental expression'. People are asked to meditate here on a theological doctrine, a particular understanding of the meaning of the last supper, and its relation to the death of Jesus, and our remembering of it until He comes.

This final mystery of light now links the joyful mysteries of Christ's hidden childhood and the luminous mysteries of his public ministry with the sorrowful and glorious mysteries of the paschal event. This is where his public ministry is leading as Luke most clearly teaches in the structure of his gospel. If it is to the paschal mystery, to 'Jerusalem', that Jesus' ministry moves it is also to 'Jerusalem', to the paschal mystery, that Christian preaching points. This is the climax and the heart of the story of Jesus of Nazareth. This is the climax and the heart of Christian preaching. This paschal mystery, sacramentally represented in the Eucharist, is described by Vatican

II as 'the source and summit of the Christian life' (*Lumen gentium* 11).

The journey to Emmaus recounted in Luke 24 is often understood as a paradigmatic Christian liturgy. The preaching, action and mission of Jesus become the preaching, action and mission of the church. There are earlier examples in the Bible of a combination of word and ritual event leading to a renewal of covenant life. Exodus 24 presents us with one of the most important of these: the law has been proclaimed to the people and the blood is sprinkled, ratifying the status of their relationship with God with the implications this now has for how they ought to live. Joshua 24 tells of a similar moment of proclamation, ritual and renewal. Other examples are 1 Kings 8, which tells of the dedication of the temple by Solomon, and Nehemiah 8–10 where we find once again proclamation and ritual event leading to a renewal in worship and right living.

In the New Testament also there are many examples of preaching leading to ritual leading to a renewal of life. Peter's preaching at Pentecost moves many of his listeners to ask 'what must we do'. The answer is that they must repent, be baptised and receive the gift of the Spirit (Acts 2:37–41). The parting words of Jesus according to Matthew's gospel commission the apostles to preach, to baptise and to teach people how to live in accordance with the gospel (Matt 28:18–20). John 6 may also be understood according to this pattern, a moment of preaching (the bread of life), a reference to the eucharist (the living bread), and implications for discipleship (do you want to go away too?). There is, we are taught, a natural flow from word to ritual to life, all three constituting a distinctive form of life, the word calling to faith, faith expressed and nourished in worship, worship bearing fruit in charity. The earliest Christians to write about preaching and worship and their interrelationship—Justin Martyr and the *Didache*, for example—show how this pattern continues as the church's 'form of life'.

Of course the great liturgy, the only true worship, is that enacted and undergone by Jesus in his suffering, death and resurrection. He is the only priest, his is the only sacrifice, he is now the temple, his is the only prayer. The signs and discourses of Jesus as recounted in the gospel of John are a prelude to the great sign, the liturgy of Calvary, through which the Spirit of divine love is poured out and the new and eternal covenant is written on the human heart. What was done by God's people beforehand in obedience to Him pointed to these events and what is done by God's people after them in obedience to Him re-presents these events.

There is not space here to trace all aspects of this rich stream through the Scriptures. It is, clearly, the heart of the matter. Let us return briefly to Luke 24, the journey to Emmaus, taking it as a paradigm of Christian liturgy to see how preaching and ritual are related there. The pilgrim community, frequently downhearted as a result of its failures in the world, needs to know that the Risen Lord has not abandoned it, but walks with it. Jesus' first concern when he meets the disciples on the road is to help them to understand the Scriptures so as to find meaning, and therefore hope and encouragement, in the events that have come upon them. Their hearts 'burn within them' as he opens to them the Scriptures. Beginning with Moses and all the prophets he explains to them the passages about himself, in particular the passages that interpret his suffering and death (Lk 24:27). What is implied is that he goes through the entire Jewish canon with them, a point that is made explicit shortly afterwards when Jesus appears to them in Jerusalem and refers to 'the law of Moses, the prophets and the psalms' (Lk 24:44). What the Torah, the prophets and the writings promised has been fulfilled in the ministry and paschal mystery of Christ. Hearts burn and minds are opened: his public ministry had been all about this, helping people to hear and to see. The great renewal liturgies of the Old Testament were about this too as is Christian preaching. But it takes the power of the paschal mystery (the Spirit of Jesus, the promise of the Father) to establish this access to truth finally and definitively.

The ritual action done by Jesus when they have arrived in Emmaus is all too familiar: 'at table with them, he took the bread and blessed, and broke it, and gave it to them' (Lk 24:30). In that moment, we are told, 'their eyes were opened and they recognised him; and he vanished out of their sight' (Lk 24:31).

Actions and words in the church's proclamation of Christ

The church continues the ministry of Jesus in the power of the Spirit—praying and healing, teaching and living in communion. It continues also to break the bread and to recognize his presence in that breaking (Acts 2:42; 1 Cor 10:16; 11:23-26). According to Mark's gospel, the centurion came to faith by witnessing the 'breaking' of Jesus:

> Jesus uttered a loud cry and breathed his last. And the curtain of the temple was torn in two, from top to bottom. And when the centurion, who stood facing him, saw that he thus breathed his last, he said, 'Truly this man was the Son of God' (Mk 15:37-39).

Notice that the tearing of the curtain from top to bottom comes between Jesus breathing his last and the centurion's response to that event. The breaking of Jesus, the breaking of the temple, the breaking of bread—it is at these limits that the transcendent mystery, present all through, is glimpsed in its disappearing. In an intriguing article Herbert McCabe reflected on this aspect of Christian experience and argued that we need a special language with which to speak appropriately of our commitment to the words, rituals and actions that make up the Christian life, if that commitment is to be full and yet leave space for qualifications and criticism.[3] This 'sacramental language' is the language of the Kingdom but only if we do not worship the sacraments themselves, he says. If Christians are to avoid their own forms of idolatry then they need a special language in which to speak of sacraments, theology and politics, a language that supports complete commitment to what is bound to fail, to what must 'break', fall away and dissolve if it is to 'reveal'.

If on one side a sacramental or ecclesiological idolatry is possible for Christians, so too is an idolatry of 'the word' when it refuses to break for the Word. What does this mean? It means that preaching too, if it is to perform its task in a way that serves Christ, must break down, it must be 'sesquiguous' to use McCabe's strange word, worthy of complete dedication on our part while we accept its relative character and its being bound to fail. As it is for liturgy and sacrament, so it is for preaching.

Preaching the Word of God is wonderful and it is terrifying. Where people talk glibly about being prophetic it is clear that they do not realise what the task involves. None of the great prophets of the Old Testament wanted the job: not Jeremiah ('too young', Jer 1:4–10), not Amos ('a tender of sycamore trees', Amos 7), not Jonah whose first reaction was to flee the presence of the Lord, and not

3 'Sacramental language', *Irish Theological Quarterly* 43 (1976): 91–103 (re-published in *God Matters* (London: Geoffrey Chapman, 1987, 165–79).

Isaiah ('a man of unclean lips', Isaiah 6). The agony of Jesus in Gethsemane shows us the Prophet of prophets contemplating where his mission has led: 'Father, all things are possible to you. Let this cup pass from me. Nevertheless not what I will but what you will' (Mk 14:36).

So the person who is too keen to be a prophet ought to arouse our suspicion. No prophet can escape the serious personal cost the job entails. There is something terrifying about this calling, to carry the Word of God to people. On one side it means talking about wonderful things like God's mercy, compassion and love. On the other it means talking about uncompromising things like God's justice, truth and judgement. The great preachers have often spent many years preparing for the task. The gospels tell us that after his hidden years Jesus spent a symbolic forty days in the wilderness, fasting and being put to the test. His preaching begins under the sign of the arrest of John the Baptist (Mk 1:12–15). Paul went to Arabia for some time after his conversion, a mysterious hiatus in his career, before he returned to become the great preacher of the gospel to the Gentiles. A similar pattern is found in the lives of other great teachers and preachers: Saint Dominic, for example, has a hidden life of ten years or so as a parish priest at Fanjeaux, after the first attempts to establish a band of preachers and before the final establishment of his Order.

A time of testing is required before a preaching mission can begin. It means searching the depths of one's own soul (to the extent that this is possible) because the Word to be carried is a double-edged sword. We are told that Christ went to preach to the spirits in prison, 'descending into hell' as the early creeds put it. To be a prophet or preacher is likely to involve a journey to hell to preach to imprisoned spirits. It means at least a battle with one's own imprisoned spirit, lest after preaching to others we find ourselves disqualified (1 Cor 9:27).

This may seem exaggerated, overly dramatic. But preachers must engage in a struggle with the Word, with the needs of people, and with themselves. They must find ways to allow those struggles to nourish their preaching, so that it will 'ring true'. The journey of God's Word through the preacher will re-enact the career of the Word of God in the world, through death in the hope of resurrection, through losing everything in the hope of gaining everything. The 'new creation', God's work in us, is only achieved through the death of the old, the 'breaking of the bread'.

The opening chapters of this book make frequent use of the metaphors of fire and light. If the Word were only light that would be one thing, but because it is also fire, the Word that breathes love in Thomas Aquinas's expression, it is guaranteed that anyone who truly handles it will get burnt. Acceptable worship, with reverence and awe, happens only when it is remembered that our God is a consuming fire (Heb 12:29; see Deut 4:24).

A particular difficulty arises when the preaching breaks down. This will be a recurring experience of the preacher, because the preaching must break down. It happened to Paul at Athens (Acts 17). It happened to Stephen just before he was stoned (Acts 7). It happened to Jesus himself, in John 6 where many decided his words were intolerable and gave up following him and in Matthew 19 where the rich young man decides it is too demanding. We must be alert for the moment of break-down not only because it is bound to happen but also because it is of great significance. We carry a heavenly treasure in earthen vessels: there is bound to be difficulty in carrying out the task. Specifically, some will find our preaching boring and irrelevant. That's not the worst of it:

some will find the preaching of the gospel objectionable, offensive, extreme, ridiculous, out-dated, a threat to common sense . . .

When Paul arrived in Corinth, it seems that he was still smarting from his experience in Athens. He came in fear and trembling, he later tells the Corinthians, knowing nothing among them except Christ crucified, not using arguments from philosophy but speaking only of the cross, a foolishness and weakness that are the wisdom and power of God. The gospel is not a wisdom of this age that is passing away. If it is for this life only that we have hoped in Christ, then we are the most unfortunate of people (1 Cor 15:19). There is a sense in which the gospel must be irrelevant to the world because it is a message that brings *new* life. It is not just an endorsement of the way things are, a pep-talk to encourage us to keep going the way we are. It is a call to transformation, the preaching seeking to bring the newness of the gospel to bear on the wisdom of every passing age. As it is in the breaking of the bread that the disciples recognized Jesus at Emmaus, so it is in the break down of the preaching that we recognize something essential to what Christian preaching is about.

Concluding comment

The Welsh Catholic poet and artist David Jones was much attached to a dictum that he found in the works of Maurice de la Taille, 'he placed himself in the order of signs' (*Epoch and Artist*, 179). The *kenosis* of the Incarnate Word extends beyond his becoming human to his death on the cross and to his translation of that event into the signs of human language and ritual action. The news of that event reaches us through the preaching of the Church, through the *praeconium* or proclamation of the great deeds of God summarised in the creeds and the great eucharistic prayers. The Christian Orthodox contribution below will explain how the New Testament itself emerged in the liturgical celebrations of the early Church. One of the great recoveries in the Roman Catholic Church in recent decades is the place and importance of the homily, recognizing that the preaching done within the liturgy is, theologically, the typical form of Christian preaching.[4] There are other opportunities of preaching the gospel, of course, but the response of the Church to the Word proclaimed in preparation for the celebration of the Sacrament is the best place to begin in thinking about the relationship between preaching and liturgy within the Christian form of life.

These introductory thoughts have been developed in response to the chapters that follow, in which the themes and arguments I have proposed, as well as many others, are considered at greater length. There are many variations within these chapters not only because everything that needs to be said cannot be said simultaneously but also because the authors speak from different theological and ecclesial backgrounds. Some of the tensions present here have, sadly, led to breaks in communion which all Christians would like to see overcome. There is also, therefore, an ecumenical hope in publishing these papers together.

The gospel has always been preached in a complex world. The present situation seems more complex and not only because it is the one in which we must live the Christian life and preach the gospel. There are today strong prejudices and arguments against the truth of any religious belief, a suspicion of anything that smacks of

4 For an excellent reflection on the place and importance of the homily see Philip Gleeson OP, 'The Homily: Serving, Not Dominating', in Vivian Boland OP, editor, *Watchmen Raise Their Voices* (Dublin: Dominican Publications, 2006), 137–44.

'preaching', and a fear that religious conviction must imply fanaticism. A comment attributed to a British member of parliament expresses well a prevalent mood: 'it seems to me that faith education works all right as long as people are not that serious about their faith' (*Sunday Independent* [Dublin] 6 January 2008). And yet Christians continue to contemplate this strange sight, that the bush is on fire but is not burnt, that human hearts continue to burn as the scriptures are opened, that many continue to recognise Him in the breaking of the word and of the bread, that many seek to follow Christ by walking in love and so imitate God (Eph 5:1–2).

1
Do Not Put Out the Burning Bush

Timothy Radcliffe OP

A friend of mine recently invited me for lunch. He is a schoolmaster and he wished me to meet some of his pupils. They were seventeen and eighteen year olds. They were wonderful, bright and beautiful. We talked about novels and films, music and food, and I felt completely at home with them. Then my friend said, 'Well, since you got on so well, next time come and preach to them about your faith'. And I had a moment of panic. What words could I find to talk about God and Jesus? If I used traditional language of faith, then it might mean nothing to them. The light would go out of their eyes. If I tried to use their language, then they might think, 'What is this old wrinkly doing pretending that he is eighteen?'

Boring and ineffectual preaching has been a problem from the very beginning. Indeed Webster's Dictionary defines to preach as, to give moral or religious advice, 'especially in a tiresome manner'. When I am discouraged by my own preaching I console myself by remembering that St Paul droned on at such length that Eutyches fell asleep and dropped to his death (Acts 20:7–12). At least so far my preaching has not killed anyone, as far as I know. Humbert of Romans talked about the preached word as sharing in God's power to raise the dead; often today it is more likely to send the living to sleep.[1] When St Caesarius of Arles preached, his sermons were so tedious that the doors had to be locked to stop the people from fleeing.

1. Simon Tugwell OP, editor, *Early Dominicans: Selected Writings* (New York: Paulist Press, 1982), 201.

John Donne, the Anglican preacher and poet, said the reason the Puritans preached for so long was that they would not stop until the congregation had woken up again!

Today we face more than the eternal problem of how not to bore the pants off people when we preach. We face a more fundamental crisis in finding words that have authority and give life. The history of the church has periodically been marked by such crises. In the thirteenth century this led to the foundation of the Dominican Order. In the fifteenth century, such a crisis resulted in the foundation of the Jesuits and in the eighteenth century, of the Redemptorists. Do not worry. I am not going to suggest that we need another religious order of preachers. Let's just stick with the Dominicans. Nor will I explore the origins of the present crisis of proclamation except to say that I suspect it is rooted in a certain sort of literalism, coming from nineteenth century scientific literalism. This can evolve either into secular ways of talking which block access to the transcendental, or to a religious fundamentalism, which storms the heavens.

I would like to reflect here on how we may find words for our faith. My approach will not be academic. I left the academic world sixteen years ago and got caught up in what is called 'leadership'. It is a word that I hate, but there we are! Instead I wish to offer a more meditative approach, pondering on two moments of silence, of inarticulacy, in the story of our faith. The first is that of Moses meeting with God in the burning bush, and the second is the Last Supper.

I will be completely honest. I had a stab at the second, the Last Supper, first, when I was asked to talk about preaching to an international meeting of Jesuits in Rome. They must have been desperate, to ask a Dominican. Someone who read this lecture asked me to come and talk about the same subject in the United States, but using a different approach. I do not know whether you have had that frustrating experience of giving a lecture which people like and so they ask you to give it again without repeating yourself. And so I tried the story of Moses as a way of exploring the challenges of preaching. This time the first will be last and I shall start with Moses and then move on to the Last Supper.

In May 2004 I was taken to the monastery of St Catherine's, at the foot of Mount Sinai. At 3.30 pm in the afternoon, when all sensible people are asleep and only 'mad dogs and Englishmen go out in the midday sun', we walked past the shrine of the burning bush and climbed the mountain of the Lord. The story of Moses may offer some clues as to how we find the words that we need. Moses is not confident that he has anything to say or that anyone will believe him. He says to God 'But behold, they will not believe me or listen to my voice, for they will say, "The Lord did not appear to you"' (Exodus 4:1), and 'Oh, my Lord, I am not eloquent, either heretofore or since thou hast spoken to thy servant; but I am slow of speech and tongue'. Then the Lord said to him, 'Who has made the human mouth? Who makes him dumb, or deaf, or seeing, or blind? Is it not I, the Lord? Therefore go and I will be with your mouth and teach you what you shall speak' (Exodus 4:10–13).

As I walked past the shrine of the burning bush, I was delighted to notice beside it a large red fire extinguisher. It looked so old that it might have been there since Moses. It seemed to symbolise our ambivalent relationship to the word that comes from the burning bush, and the perpetual temptation to quench it.

When one talks about one's faith, the hardest thing is to find the first word. How can one break the silence? In the old days of typewriters, I would type a sentence and then tear up the paper and type just the same sentence again. Soon the floor would be covered with ripped up pages, with almost identical words.

When I was a student in Paris, my hero was Michel Foucault. I went to every lecture of his. I did not understand much, but I was convinced that I was on the edge of revelation. When he gave his first lecture in the Collège de France, this is how he began:

> 'Rather than open with a word, I would have wished to be enveloped by it, and be carried beyond every possible beginning. I would have liked to discover, at the moment of speaking, a voice without name preceding me for a long time: it would have been enough for me to tag along, to follow the phrase, to nestle myself, without care, in its interstices, as if she had beckoned to me in holding herself, for an instant, in suspense.'[2]

Moses finds the Word waiting for him in the wilderness. In the beginning was the Word. Our words never break the silence, but respond to the word that precedes us. Annie Dillard tells of a rabbi, Shmelke of Nickolsburg, who appears to have been rather a nuisance. Every time his teacher, the Maggid of Mezritch, began to preach he would say 'The Lord spoke'. And Shmelke would get carried away, and just go on shouting, 'The Lord, spoke, The Lord spoke' until they had to carry him out of the room and dump him somewhere until he cooled off![3]

Whatever silent wilderness we may inhabit, we know that the Lord has spoken. There is a word that is waiting for us in the desert. All we can do is share the encounter. The word is looking for us. It is like a heat seeking missile.

---

2. *L'Ordre du Discours: Leçon Inaugurale au Collège de France* (Paris: Gallimard, 1971), 7 (my translation).
3. *The Writing Life* (New York: Harper and Row, 1990), 35.

If we expose any part of our humanity and vulnerability, then it will seek us out.

Moses meets the God of his ancestors, of Abraham, Isaac and Jacob. But he does not know this God's name. It is as if Moses and the Israelites are suffering from religious amnesia. They have forgotten the God of their ancestors, who made promises. The transmission of the memory of the promise has been broken.

This is a pretty accurate description of our crisis of proclamation today. In Europe, and I suspect in Australia though not so much in the United States, we are suffering from that failure of memory. Parents have found it hard to transmit the language of faith to their children. This is symbolised by the often-repeated story of the person who goes to buy a cross, and asks for the one with the little man on it. I once instructed in the faith a bright young man of Imperial College, London and on one occasion, detecting some confusion, I asked him what he knew of Moses. He said, 'Well, the name rings a bell. Wasn't he one of the nastier devils that Jesus expelled?'

This also means that we have forgotten the promise of the land flowing with milk and honey. As Francis Fukuyama said, history is ended. The only story we can tell of the future is the war on terrorism. Moses goes back to Egypt to awaken the hope of the Promised Land. The God of whom I would wish to talk with these bright young teenagers is the God of hope. That is the fundamental challenge for us, to find a language of hope. But we are more radically confronted with that in the Last Supper, and so I will return to that theme in my second essay in this collection.[4] Let's leave it aside for the moment.

God discloses his name to Moses, a name usually translated 'I am who I am' (Exodus 3:14). It is a strange

---

4. Chapter 7 below, 'This is My Body, Given For You'.

name, and we do not even know how it was pronounced. It reveals God and conceals him at the same time. In our tradition it has usually been seen as a sort of metaphysical revelation. Moses meets the God who exists absolutely, the God of pure being. But this all sounds rather Greek, and our God is the God of Abraham rather than Aristotle. Many of you are surely more familiar with speculation about its meaning than I am, but I have the impression that it is now more usually seen as a dynamic title; 'I will be whom I will be', or even 'I will cause to be what I will cause to be'. Moses encounters a sort of religious Big Bang.

One of my Dominican brethren who influenced me most was Cornelius Ernst. He was born in Sri Lanka. His father was Dutch Anglican and his mother was a Sri Lankan Buddhist. Cornelius became a Communist when he was at Colombo University but was thrown out of the party for his free-thinking. He went to Cambridge where he studied under Wittgenstein and became known as a budding poet. He became a Catholic as the only way of holding all this together. One of his fundamental intuitions was that at the heart of Christianity was what he called 'the genetic moment', the happening of grace. To see the truth of things, to open our eyes to reality, is to glimpse the happening of things. He wrote,

> the budding is more illuminatingly the moment of the real than the flower or the soil out of which it grows'. A daffodil is not so much a yellow object as a sort of happening of yellow-ness. 'Every genetic moment is a mystery. It is dawn, discovery, spring, new birth, coming to the light, awakening, transcendence, liberation, ecstasy, bridal consent, gift, forgiveness, reconciliation, revolution, faith, hope, love. It could be said that Christianity is the

> consecration of the genetic moment, the living centre from which it reviews the indefinitely various and shifting perspectives of human experience in history. That, at least, is or ought to be its claim: that it is the power to transform and renew all things: 'Behold I make all things new' (Revelation 21:5).[5]

Meeting God is not like encountering a very powerful person. Encountering the burning bush is not like meeting an invisible President Bush. Sinai is not Fort David. It is the experience of grace. So the sharing of our faith is a sharing in this happening of novelty, of renewal, of transformation. Of course we do share truths, such as that God is one and three, that Jesus is divine and human, and that he was raised from the dead. But these are not plodding, mundane facts, like that I am English or that the world is round. They are explosive, grace filled. In a novel by a young American called Leif Enger, *Peace like a River*, a young kid asks about a preacher, 'Do things happen when he preaches?'[6] Preaching is trying to share in those explosive moments of liberation, when something new happens.

Moses sees this burning bush and he is intrigued. He goes to investigate. 'I will turn aside and see this great sight, why the bush is not burnt.' The encounter begins with puzzlement. And so our entry into any scriptural text always begins not so much with 'what does it say?' as with 'what is happening here?' We can see how a text may be a happening of grace most clearly with the parables. They shock us into a new perception. If we hear

5. *The Theology of Grace* [*Theology Today* Number 17] (Notre Dame Indiana: Fides, 1974), 74–75.
6. (London: Atlantic Monthly Press, 2001), 38.

the parable of the Pharisee and the publican, then we need to be shaken by its conclusion. We need to catch with the whiff of scandal when Jesus says that it is the sinner who goes home justified. If we are already reaching for that conclusion when we read the text, then something may fail to happen. We will have to work hard to recapture the event of the parable. In that way scriptural texts are like jokes. The joke is the event of laughter, and if you know the punch line already then you are unlikely to laugh, unless you are caught by the infection of another's laugh. In hearing someone else laugh in surprise, we may be captured again by the initial shock. When we preach, then sometimes it is the astonishment of our listeners that reawakens the text for us.

This is why it is so hard to preach on well-known texts. I dread weddings at which one has to preach on 1 Corinthians 13. The handkerchiefs are already out before hardly a word is spoken. I love to be asked to speak on hard texts, like why women must wear hats in church or on Edom as God's wash-bowl. I remember the pleasure of being asked to preach at a wedding on the text, 'There is a time for gathering stones and a time for throwing them away'. The sort of happening to be spotted depends, of course, on the genre of the text. A legal text will rarely scandalise us immediately. We will have to discover what it replaces, what is initiated or renounced. 'An eye for an eye' is only a grace-filled event if we see it as the renunciation of unlimited revenge. In a text from the priestly tradition of the Old Testament we may need to glimpse the happening of order in a world of chaos.

A Jewish rabbi told this story about his grandfather, who was a pupil of the famous rabbi Baal Shem Tov. He said,

> My grandfather was paralysed. Once he was asked to tell a story about his teacher and he told how the holy Baal Shem Tov

> used to jump and dance when he was praying. My grandfather stood up while he was telling the story and the story carried him away so much that he had to jump and dance to show how the master had done it. From that moment he was healed. This is how stories ought to be told.[7]

So preaching is the sharing of the happening of grace. This need not be in words. The most moving Christmas vigil that I have ever attended was in Paris in 1995. It was a Christmas Mass for tramps, celebrated in a big tent in the centre of Paris. The priest was a Spanish Dominican, Pedro Meca, who lives like a tramp on the streets of Paris and comes back to his brethren just once a week for a shower and a big meal. I think the brethren hope he has the shower before the meal! All the destitute, the homeless, and the bums were invited to the Mass. A thousand came. It was a celebration of intense if sometimes befuddled happiness. The altar was made of cardboard, to celebrate the Christ who was born for all those who live in cardboard boxes today. When Pedro pulled the cork of the wine bottle at the offertory, cheers rang out. Afterwards everyone was invited to a superb banquet. That was a sign of the Kingdom. That was a gesture that reached across the divisions of rich and poor and spoke of the joy of the Kingdom. Something happened that night that opened the door to what happened two thousand years ago.

It is so helpful that we are told the story of Moses' encounter with the burning bush. He does not know what to make of it. Every preaching surely begins with puzzlement, with incomprehension. 'What is going on here?'

---

7. Martin Buber, quoted by Johann Baptist Metz, 'A Short Apology of Narrative', in *Concilium* 5/9 (May 1973): 86–7.

The beginning of our preaching is embracing that incomprehension, sharing humanity's silence in the face of the gospel. Barbara Brown Taylor wrote that

> (i)n each of the gospels, the Word comes forth from silence. For John, it is the silence at the beginning of creation. For Luke, it is the silence of poor old Zechariah, struck dumb by the angel Gabriel for doubting that Elizabeth would bear a child. For Matthew, it is the awkward silence between Joseph and Mary when she tells him her prenuptial news. And for Mark, it is the voice of one crying in the wilderness—the long-forgotten voice of prophecy puncturing the silence of the desert and of time.[8]

Mark above all is the gospel of silence, culminating in the silence of Jesus on the cross and ending originally with the silence of the women as they flee from the tomb, 'and they said nothing to anyone, for they were afraid' (Mark 16:8).

We must let ourselves be silenced by the text, not knowing what it means, letting it escape our mastery and possession. It is the word that we cannot domesticate and tame. We must not reach for the fire extinguisher. We will have nothing to say until we find that we do have nothing to say. Then we turn to God and beg for a word. Dominic wished that the Order of Preachers be a community of beggars.

The word that we are to preach may be given in a moment. Einstein compared having a new idea to a chicken laying an egg: '*Keeks—auf einmal ist es da*',

8. *When God is Silent* (Boston: Cowley Publications, 1998), 73.

'cheep—and all at once there it is'.[9] Czeslaw Milosz said of great poems that they spring into our presence and stand there, blinking and lashing their tails, like little tigers.[10] Most of us are not like Einstein or Milosz and we have to struggle to understand. The sharing of the struggle is part of the preaching. The bringing to birth of the word is what we share with our hearers, often that which is most important. We are with them, modern men and women who are puzzled, labouring to understand, awaiting the gift of insight. Annie Dillard captures well the combination of gift and hard grind that is involved in all creative writing:

> At its best, the sensation of writing is that of any unmerited grace. It is handed to you, but only if you look for it. You search, you break your heart, your back, your brain and then—and only then—it is handed to you. From the corner of your eye you can see motion. Something is moving the air and headed your way.[11]

The words that appear effortlessly, like Einstein's chicken's egg, may seem to be too polished and finished for our hearers. The preaching is not so much the announcement of the good news as the sharing of its gift, and God usually gives through our beating our heads against the limits of our understanding. As William Hill OP wrote, 'God cannot do without the stammering ways

---

9. Quoted by Annie Dillard in *Writing Life* (New York: Harper and Row 1990), 76.
10. Quoted by Seamus Heaney in *The Redress of Poetry* (London: Faber and Faber, 1995), 127.
11. *Ibid*, 75.

in which we strive to give utterance to [the] Word'.[12] Our stuttering words can speak more than well-rounded phrases because they are those of someone receiving a gift rather than demonstrating his own richness.

We begin with the silence, then the struggle, and then often there is granted an astonishing word. We share that astonishment. The novelist Louise Erdrich describes herself as 'a writer only, a woman constantly surprised'.[13] The preacher may share that constant surprise. As Rabbi Abraham Joshua Herchel said, 'Lord, I did not ask for success; I asked for wonder and you gave it to me.' The word is given. As Yann Martel writes in *The Life of Pi*: 'No thundering from a pulpit, no condemnation from bad churches, no peer pressure, just a book of scriptures quietly waiting to say hello, as gentle and powerful as a little girl's kiss on your cheek'.[14]

The encounter of Moses with the burning bush is also to do with power. God promises powerful deeds. Moses will confront Pharaoh, inflict Egypt with the plagues, and lead the people to freedom and the Promised Land. God promises a 'regime change' in Canaan. The animation of our preaching implies that our words acquire something of that liberating power. But despite all the terrible deeds that God will do there is already the hint that this power ultimately is a sort of weakness and vulnerability.

For a start God tells Moses his own name. The gods were very hesitant about telling anyone their true names, for that meant placing themselves in the mouths and so in the power of those who knew their names. God's

---

12. William Hill OP, 'Preaching as a "Moment" in Theology', in Mary Catherine Hilkert OP, editor, *Search for the Absent God*, New York: Crossroad, 1992), 186, quoted by Paul Janowiak, *The Holy Preaching: The Sacramentality of the Word in the Liturgical Assembly* (Collegeville: Liturgical Press, 2000), 187.
13. *The Blue Jay's Dance: A Birth Year* (London: HarperCollins, 1995), x.
14. *The Life of Pi* (Edinburgh: Canongate, 2002), 208.

revelation of his name is a first tiptoe into the vulnerability of Jesus at the Last Supper, when he will place himself in our hands. The Jews were so deeply aware of the scandal of the self-disclosure of the name that the name was increasingly protected, hedged around by rules, until it could only be pronounced by the High Priest once a year, and then when the sounding of trumpets made it inaudible. This name finds clear enunciation in the name 'Jesus', 'Yahweh saves'.

It is above all Moses who must become vulnerable, giving up the security of the wilderness, the safety of his new family, and returning to Egypt where his life is sought. He must confront Pharaoh. 'Who am I that I should go to Pharaoh and bring out the children of Egypt' (Exodus 3:11). I wonder whether our proclamation of our faith sounds so flat and unconvincing because it is not marked by that vulnerability, that struggle with doubt, that personal exposure and risk. People need to see that the encounter with the gospel has passed through our fragility, our messy, faulted humanity. The sharing of our faith implies a self-disclosure. Our names are, as it were, placed in the mouths of other people, nakedly.

Being preachers must reshape our humanity, deconstruct our masks, and give us faces that reveal. Simon Tugwell put it beautifully at the end of *The Way of the Preacher*:

> The man [please overlook any sexism] who is both a preacher and a brother can learn, painfully and probably with uneven progress, what it means to be a face for God precisely in having a human face, a face which can smile and laugh and weep and look bored. God's self-expression in his preaching does not over-ride or render superfluous the expression of his own

> creaturely identity. The way in which he must have the courage to be seen both by those with whom he lives and by those to whom he preaches, will at least indicate to him the necessity and the possibility of a convergence between what he is in himself and what he is as an expression of God's Word. And these two are not really two. It is in all our uniqueness and individuality, which is eternally valid and desired by God, that we are also the revelation, the manifestation, the expression of him who is the One Word coming forth from all eternity from the silence of the Father.[15]

The sharing of one's own struggles and doubts can sound rather self-centred, as if the preacher were the good news. And it is a temptation for preachers to make themselves the centre of attention. I heard of one famous English Dominican preacher in the last century who could dazzle a congregation with the whirl of his cappa. There was a thirteenth century Italian Dominican, John of Vicenza, who was such a star that when he went to have his hair cut, people fought over possession of the clippings of his hair, as if they were relics. In fact he was irritated with his brethren who, typically, refused to join in the cult![16]

But it is only if we speak in our own voices, as the men and the women that we are, that people may recognise the good news, the happening of grace. As Barbara Brown Taylor wrote, 'When I speak out of my humanity, I want

---

15. *The Way of the Preacher* (London: Darton, Longman & Todd 1979), 96.
16. Augustine Thompson OP, *Revival Preachers and Politics in Thirteenth Century Italy: The Great Devotion of 1233* (Oxford: Oxford University Press, 1992), 129.

my listeners to recognise their own. When I say "I", I want them to say "Me too".' If they catch my doubts, hesitations, struggles and surprises and delight, then they will recognise their own. If it passes through the prism of my own complexity, tested and found true there, then, paradoxically it is more likely that I will disappear from the scene, and it is the happening of grace that will be spotted. This is true whether it is a middle-aged person speaking to the young, or an English person speaking to Indians—or even to Australians! This is why the inculturation of the gospel is not divisive. My experience is that when we truly speak out of the cultures that are our own then we are recognisable as brothers and sisters, born of the same Word. It is when we seek to speak in some pseudo-universal tongue that wide spaces are opened up between us.

Moses must confront Pharaoh. The preacher must inevitably come into conflict with the powers that be. How can we do this, who belong to the powerful West? What does this mean for us now, who are living at this turning point in humanity's history, under the shadow of 9/11, when all that the future promises is more violence and the clash of religions? There can be no powerful word unless we confront the ways in which we are implicated in the exercise of oppressive power, whether within the Church or as members of society. Karl Barth wrote that to call these texts of the Bible 'the Word of God' is to claim they 'resist every attempt at colonization and all forms of hegemony'.[17] Their power is to liberate us from all the false powers that suffocate human beings, all the little Pharaohs that hold us in bondage. And this is not just an economic and military power but that of our great export

17. TJ Gorringe *Furthering Humanity: A Theology of Culture* (Aldershot: Ashgate, 2004), 118.

which is so-called cultural productions. John Baptist Metz argued that

> for a long time non-western countries have been under siege from a 'second colonization': through the invasion of the Western culture industry and its mass media, especially that of television, which holds people prisoner in an artificial world, a world of make-believe. It alienates them more and more from own cultural images, from their original language and their own history. This colonization of the spirit is so much harder to resist because it appears as a sugar coated poison and because the gentle terror of this Western culture industry operates not as an alienation but as a narcotic drug.[18]

Finally, this encounter of Moses with God suggests the happening of home. 'Come, I will send you to Pharaoh, that you may bring forth the children of Israel out of Egypt.' Preaching summons people out of whatever small prisons they may inhabit, into the wide-open spaces of God. The preacher is like the Good Shepherd whose voice invites the sheep to leave the tight, little pens in which they are stuck and come out into the vastness of God where they belong. Our words must not just talk about that wide-open space; they must create it, let it happen. Words of grace are the happening of home. Again this is a theme which finds a much more radical articulation in the event of the Last Supper and let us consider it in that context.

---

18. In H Regan and A Torrance, editors, *Christ and Context* (Edinburgh: T&T Clark, 1993), 212, quoted in Gorringe, *op.cit*, 85.

So I must stop now. I have been trying to suggest that our words about God will only recover power if we see preaching not as the presentation of facts so much as the happening of grace. 'Does anything happen when he preaches?' The story of the burning bush gives us some preliminary hints as to what sort of happening that might be. We have to discover the text as eventful, and recover our astonishment at what happens. It is a power that ultimately asks of the preacher vulnerability, a sort of nakedness. It is the happening of home. This may sound rather Protestant. I think that when we look at the Last Supper, then we shall go a little bit deeper and discover what theologians like Karl Rahner and Edward Schillebeeckx call the sacramentality of the Word.

2
Kindlers of Fire, Lighters of Firebrands

Elaine Farmer

Preaching has a bad name. The word's reputation, in English at least, is pretty shabby. The same goes for 'sermon'. Whatever great heights these two companions have reached in past centuries, and regardless of any current value they may occasionally achieve, in the wider world whose opinion shapes our language, they are not valued at all. They have come to mean boredom, 'being talked down to', being told what to do or how to behave, being criticised, 'moralised at' and generally put down. 'He's always preaching at us!' 'I don't need another sermon from her!' 'What an awful 'preachy' voice!' 'Sermonising again!' So it goes on. Even 'practise what you preach' can quickly acquire a suspiciously negative imperative tone. Some of the great lyrical and inspirational writing in English has come from the pens of the church's preachers but 'preaching' and 'sermon', poor things, are like two precious birds that have escaped from the church's coop only to discover that freedom without nurture is not life but death; to be sullied and brought low by an alien world that does not care whether they live or die.

But the church ought to care. Preaching is central to its *raison d'être*: to proclaim the Gospel of Christ. *'The Lord God has given me the tongue of a teacher, that I may know how to sustain the weary with a word'*, the writer of the third servant song of Isaiah calls to us. *'Who among you fears the Lord and obeys the voice of his servant, who walks in darkness and has no light, yet trusts in the name of the Lord and relies upon his God? But all of you are kindlers of fire, lighters of firebrands. Walk in the flame of your fire, and among the brands that you have kindled!*[1] One of the great writers on homiletics called Isaiah's words—*kindlers of fire* and *lighters of firebrands*—'a motto for poetry, a judgment of poetry' and concluded, rightly I think, that 'what is a motto for poetry could also be one for preaching'.[2] For Isaiah's words remind us of two of our goals as preachers: to comfort our hearers, but also to direct them to God through Christ. We might note, rather ruefully I confess, that Isaiah next says, *This is what you shall have from my hand: you shall lie down in torment.*[3] Many, it seems, have felt that that sums up their experience of preaching in a word: torment. Those two precious birds have not always been nurtured well within the church. As often as not, they have been fed a diet of ignorance, carelessness and sloth, and their feathers are falling out through neglect.

What to do? I want to consider that question from a practical perspective, the particular perspective of those on the receiving end, the people in the pews, and to discuss some implications of their opinions. At St Mark's National Theological Centre in Canberra, in the homiletical training of candidates for ordination within the Anglican Church,[4] we began to invite lay people to tell us what it is like to listen to preachers in church on

---

1. Isaiah 50:10–11a.
2. REC Browne, *The Ministry of the Word* (London: SCM Press, 1958), 23.
3. Isaiah 50:11b.
4. The St Mark's Diploma of Anglican Orders is now a required qualification for candidates for ordination in the Anglican Diocese of Canberra and Goulburn, and in a number of other dioceses. One semester of the two-year program is devoted to homiletics. The other three semesters address in turn the Anglican Ordinal, prayer and spirituality, and ethical issues in ministry.

Sunday.[5] We seek a reasonably broad spread of opinion[6] and this year we invited, first, a retired male university professor who has been a worshipping Anglican all his life. The second respondent was a female public servant in her 30's with an academic background in classics and literature, a doctorate in ancient history, a masters degree with honours in international law, and who is an interested and acute observer of the world of religion and worship. The third was a middle-aged male historian experienced in interpretation theory and presentation of material in public venues such as museums and galleries. He is a practising Anglican with a Quaker background. Finally, we invited a young woman in her early 20's, the daughter of an Anglican priest, who has listened to many preachers as she has grown up and who brought to us the invaluable critique of one with nostalgic affection for the church but who also belongs to a mostly disaffected young generation. By and large, the verdict of these lay people was not encouraging. They have all encountered moments of passion, glory and grace—but rarely. Too often, they have encountered only inadequate scholarly preparation, turgid and lacklustre presentation and, consequently for them, boredom and irritation. Their verdict reminded me of the old joke about Wagner: wonderful moments and terrible half hours.

---

5. I am conscious that many lay people preach, but this paper arises from the context of clergy training and therefore looks at preaching from within that perspective.
6. This small group was carefully chosen but four people do not make a statistical sample. We chose people who we knew would be articulate, intelligent and honest in their critique. There is no suggestion that they represent a social or educational cross section of Anglican churchgoers nor that others might not hold different views. Our aim in part was to ensure critique that would guarantee discussion, even controversy, rather than nurture comfort.

First, a word or two about preaching in the modern world. Conflicting theologies of preaching, social theories, cultural mores, the breakdown of old beliefs, and the growth of individualism and relativism are all relevant to this topic but discussion of them is beyond the limits of a short paper. Nevertheless, it seems reasonable to begin with the premise that preachers live in, and must therefore contend with, a world more interested in sound bites than reasoned listening, immediate pleasure (often voyeuristic and vicarious) than the bracing discomfort of the gospel[7] and clear cut solutions than hard won spiritual exercise. The word 'contend' alone signals troubled homiletical times. The negative or indifferent attitude of 'the world' certainly makes *The Macquarie Dictionary*'s definition of 'contend'—to struggle in opposition, to strive in rivalry, to compete—a pertinent description of the modern preacher's task. Even when one reads on and considers the somewhat less adversarial definitions of 'contend'—to strive in debate, to dispute earnestly—the sense of an uphill task is hardly lessened.

At the same time, a harsh judgment by 'the church' of 'the world' as cold, rejecting and selfishly self-absorbed is not entirely fair. It suggests, first, a separation of world and church that equates world with sin and sinfulness and church with sinless-ness, a distinction I strongly reject. 'The church' laments and wrings its hands over empty pews and the indifference of an apparently wayward world but absence from church is not a matter of sinful wilfulness. Second, an entirely negative judgment of the world by the church assumes that rejection of the church means lack of interest in matters spiritual. This, too, is an unacceptable assumption. The plethora of spiritual philosophies and gurus leading

---

7. Aidan Kavanagh, *Elements of Rite: A Handbook of Liturgical Style* (New York: Pueblo Publishing Company, 1982), 21.

profitable existences, in the modern western world at least, suggests that lack of interest is not the problem.

Perhaps it could be argued that we can be certain of none of this, that such remarks are merely subjective opinions and untested assumptions but the one thing I think we can assume with certainty is that nobody is interested in being bored. On the part of those with some church experience, non-attendance is, at least in part, a matter of judgment against a less than edifying product. Why would one bother to go to hear a barren offering from the pulpit, let alone return for more? On the part of those without any church experience, why would people seek the spiritual perspective on life the Christian church offers at all, given that the sermon is an alien beast and preaching just a synonym for boredom? It seems a thankless task to preach at all confronted by such wholesale reluctance yet that is the task. 'I saw myself as a fool shouting a folly to a heedless world,' Morris West has the pope say in one of his novels. 'So be it!' he continued, 'that is what we preach: transcendent nonsense which we trust in the end will make a divine logic'.[8]

The opinions expressed by the lay respondents at St Mark's provided an important broad-ranging critique and, at the same time, demonstrated the high degree of intelligence and education facing preachers from the pews, and being brought to bear on their product. The overall verdict was uncompromising: 'near enough is not good enough'. They demand not only evidence of attention by preachers to the hard work of preparation and presentation of sermons, but also evidence of attention by preachers to their own souls. The underlying implication of their critique is that preachers have an obligation to ongoing personal education and spiritual development, that the church has an obligation to be

8. *The Shoes of the Fisherman* (London: Heinemann, 1973), 186.

scrupulous about those to whom it gives its *imprimatur* to preach, and that both obligations are clearly viewed by those in the pews as imperatives for the sake of the gospel.

The issue of authority emerged as of prime importance, albeit with a difference. 'Take authority to preach the word of God,' the ordaining bishop says to new priests in the Anglican ordination service[9] but the authority of the church, it seems, is not necessarily sufficient to impress all listeners with the claims of 'biblical authority', and automatic acceptance of words spoken 'in the name of God'. 'Your authority as a preacher is based entirely on the quality of your sermon as I perceive it from the pew', said one lay respondent.[10] From more than one person came the observation that the preacher's position in the church hierarchy does not matter at all. What matters is hard evidence of the hard yards behind sermons and whether they, the hearers, encounter grace as a result. 'People's perceptions become your reality',[11] we were told. They are the basis of the preacher's legitimacy, not his or her job or title or position in the church.

'Hard evidence of the hard yards' translates into hearing sermons of substance. Substance begins with its being clear that preachers have something to say, that they have actually wrestled with difficulties and paradoxes, that they have not pushed 'the untidy bits' out of sight behind a convenient pile of little-used books, that they have not resorted to *clichés* and 'fluffy, sugar-plum platitudes', and that they have not insulted the

9. *An Australian Prayer Book* (Sydney: Broughton Books, 1995), 797.
10. Dr Ada Cheung, unpublished paper, '"What is Truth?": Legitimacy 101, or Preaching Without Due Care and Attention', St Mark's National Theological Centre, Canberra,19 March 2004, 3.
11. Cheung, *loc.cit.*

intelligence of congregations with what one person called 'the lectionary for dummies'. This latter objection translates into a demand that preachers remember that increasing numbers of their hearers are likely to be theologically educated[12] and, even if they are not, that they are astute enough to see the obvious in bible readings. Consequently, they do not want statements of the obvious. They do not want uninspired and uninspiring lectures jerking awkwardly from reading to reading like slack-jointed puppets. They do want imaginative, interesting and challenging explorations of the possible implications of the bible texts for their lives. They are asking that preachers be what James A Wallace calls 'mediator[s] of meaning' to 'a people hungry, sometimes desperately so, for meaning in their lives'.[13]

Our lay respondents were outspoken about the need for preachers to see life and death, hope and despair, God and grace, as their 'core business' but not as abstract concepts. They are looking for sermons that dive into the mess and chaos of living rather than ignoring its contradictions. They do not want to be told only—and yet again—about a god who loves them despite their sin and suffering. They want to hear about the God who is at the heart of that suffering. They know that to live is to know ambivalence and their minds and souls tell them that somewhere in that ambivalence, God is. They want

---

12. The high number of committed lay people pursuing theological education, and without any intention of seeking ordination, bears witness to this assertion. The popularity of the four-year Education for Ministry (EFM) program means there are many parishes where substantial numbers of lay people view sermons through a more finely tuned theological lens than in earlier decades when many of today's preachers were trained.
13. James A Wallace, *Preaching to the Hungers of the Heart. The Homily on the Feasts and within the Rites* (Collegeville: Liturgical Press, 2002), ix.

sermons that explore real life as it is lived and experienced and not as some kind of ideal unreality. They want their lives taken seriously, respected and addressed. They want to hear sermons that explore doubt, not deny its existence.

From those for whom doubt is the principal reality, the challenge to preachers is perhaps the most powerful. In what is yet another warning to preachers against complacency, identification among our lay respondents at this point came from the heart of the preacher's own world, in words from one of Paul Tillich's great sermons. We can't afford to forget or ignore the fact that in modern congregations many are familiar with the preacher's classic texts (as well as the bible) and relate strongly to Tillich's words about agnostics 'who have not received . . . the Spirit' of which Paul wrote in his Letter to the Romans. Excusing the linguistic exclusivity of Tillich's day, they count themselves in communion with Tillich's doubters who yet seek to understand:

> [Paul] tells us that . . . we must not believe that the Spirit is far from us . . . Our sighing in the depth of our souls, which we are not able to articulate, is taken by God to be the work of the Spirit within us. To the man who longs for God and cannot find Him; to the man who wants to be acknowledged by God and cannot even believe that He is; to the man who is striving for a new and imperishable meaning of his life and cannot discover it—to this man Paul speaks. We are each such a man.[14]

---

14. Paul Tillich 'Witness of the Spirit', in *The Shaking of the Foundations* (London: SCM Press, 1957), 139 (sermon on Romans 8:1–16, 26–7)

Paradoxically perhaps, the hope expressed at this point was the most poignant, and the demands made of preachers the most respectful. The fact that people who name themselves agnostic, or even atheist, come to listen, and most carefully, to the preacher's words, is something to be treated with great tenderness and profound respect. There is in their coming at all a desire to hear something that justifies an embryonic hope, a desire to believe that the God, whom they cannot find, is. The tension between addressing the gathered community of the faithful and addressing curious 'outsiders' who wander into the church's 'strongholds' was well appreciated. Preachers must necessarily speak to the concerns of their particular congregations but they also need to throw their homiletic nets wide, provided they are carried only by sufficient evangelistic weights to intrigue, not to repel, those who wonder if they might want to be caught in the net.

After all, our respondents reminded us, there are competitors in the field when it comes to exploring the human condition and to providing comfort and hope to live by. 'I expect a preacher to illuminate insights into the human condition that I can't get from poetry or history,' was one challenge. 'Tell me what's in the parable of the Prodigal Son that isn't in *King Lear*?'[15] The power of Shakespeare is his ability through his characters to reflect to us who we are, to challenge us with our own disconcerting contradictions, secret sins and desires. If, as preachers, we want to survive this kind of competition, we must do precisely that, leaving listeners to draw their own lessons for themselves from this exposure, rather than having their thinking done for them. Dictatorial harangues will never win the minds and hearts of those who long for God. Nor are they good for the preacher's soul though many an ego is happy to flirt with the

15. Cheung, *op cit*, 5.

powerful attractions of the dictator's way. 'The habit of haranguing is in itself pernicious,' says one writer. 'I have known even the conscientious and pious, the humane and liberal dried up by it into egoism and vanity, and have watched the mind, growing black and rancid in its own smoke.'[16]

Our respondents pushed us towards unsafe ground here. Dictatorial means may be inappropriate and people may well not want to be told what to think but we nevertheless have a word to speak about 'God's word of salvation, hope, healing, and liberation'.[17] Yes, we should respect people's desire to do their own thinking but, at the same time, we are called to 'name grace'.[18] Somewhere we need to find a path down from the very high 'mountain top' view of preaching of such as Rudolf Bultmann ('preaching itself belongs to the fact of salvation . . . this fact [is] not what it is without the preaching'[19]) and of Phillips Brooks (preaching is 'the communication of truth by man to men'[20])—we need to find a path down from the mountain top to the plains and a world dancing with its golden calves. A postmodern world that says 'my golden calf is as good as your golden calf' will have no truck with assumptions about truth. It rejects the notion there is any universal word of truth that we can speak and

---

16. Walter Savage Landor, *Uncollected Essays,* Dial Essays 1841, found at the following website: http://emersoncentral.com/waltersavage_landor.htm
17. Mary Catherine Hilkert, *Naming Grace: Preaching and the Sacramental Imagination* (New York: Continuum, 1997), 48.
18. Hilkert, *op cit,* 48–9.
19. Rudolf Bultmann, *Existence and Faith: Shorter Writings of Rudolf Bultmann*, translated by Schubert M Ogden (London: Hodder & Stoughton, 1960), 79.
20. Phillips Brooks, late eighteenth century Episcopal Bishop of Boston, quoted in John F Thornton & Katharine Washburn, *Tongues of Angels. Tongues of Men: A Book of Sermons* (London: Doubleday Books, 1999), 3.

retaliates with the assertion that no word from God can be listened to or considered unless it conforms to preconceived preferences. This does not mean that preachers should prostitute Christ's gospel by striking populist poses in the pulpit. Nor does it mean abandoning the merits of a high view of preaching. It means remembering that Moses met God on the mountain and God forgave the people for what was happening on the plain.[21] It means that, like Moses', our faces should shine at encountering God[22] on the mountain but that we should speak of how God is already active on the plain. We might argue the toss on this—it is not a new debate—but, unless we speak well enough to catch its ears and have it listen, the world we want to hear what we have to say will stare us down, shrug its shoulders and go elsewhere to explore 'what is truth?' with others. Loud voices will not catch its ears; intelligent preparation and shared vulnerability will, for some at least.

The male historian echoed the other respondents' comments in his hope for sermons that are not 'closed circles', that is, he wants sermons that do not begin and end in the Bible without taking a look at the weather in the world outside. What's more, he added, sermons should allow ambiguity. 'Help me, Lord, in my unbelief'—his paraphrase of Mark 9:24—is the cry that no amount of passionate conviction about the revelation of God-in-scripture will wipe out. He would, I think, agree with Bultmann's view: 'Revelation encounters man [sic] in the word—in the word that sounds forth *in his present*.'[23] He spoke about his experience of mounting historical exhibitions and trying to present material in a way that

21 . Exodus 32:14.

22. Exodus 34:29.

23. Rudolf Bultmann, *op cit*, 9. My italics.

would engage visitors.[24] There are, he pointed out, two types of audience, captive and voluntary. People will tolerate the former if they have a clear motive such as a job requirement, the need for certification or money. With such things in mind they will put up with dull uninspiring presentations even if they are bored. They attend, and stay, because of the reward involved.

A voluntary audience, on the other hand, is more likely to be motivated by interest or self-enrichment. They can leave any time they want and no external rewards are involved. Preachers address voluntary audiences such as these despite the question that might be raised about whether 'a reward in heaven' fits the category of 'external rewards'. I suggest though that, if preachers are relying on a rewards and punishment approach to attract or retain congregations, they are peddling a theology of fear of a punitive God, an angry Big-Daddy-in-Heaven (not to mention an angry Mother God) ready and waiting to deal with anyone who steps out of line, and that such theology is not only outdated but useless, and especially in a questioning, educated and sceptical world.

The formula proposed by interpretation theorists is, this historian suggested, particularly useful to preachers: presentations should be enjoyable, relevant (that is, meaningful and personal), organised and thematic. If we extend the formula to include 'imaginative' and 'concise', we have the teasing acronym of **EROTIC** as a guiding principle for preaching.[25] Some theorists speculate that teaching and presenting material so people retain

---

24. He drew on the seminal work of American communications specialist, Freeman Tilden, suggesting that Tilden's interpretation theory for presenting exhibitions applies equally well to preaching. For Tilden's work see Freeman Tilden, *Interpreting Our Heritage*, third edition (Chapel Hill: The University of North Carolina Press, 1977).
25. This formula is drawn from the work of another American communications specialist, Sam Ham.

information is about triggering 'the dopamine factor', that is the alleged release of the chemical, dopamine, in the brain when a person experiences pleasurable events.[26] In general, collections of facts do not engage; story telling relating to a clear theme does. If people are entertained or engaged they will attend and remember; if they are bored they will not attend without some highly significant personal motive for doing so, as we've just noted. It is interesting at this point to see that the Uniting Church in Victoria has recently released the results of a survey of what their congregations think of their clergy. Twenty-five per cent of those surveyed judged their clergy to be failures as preachers. The Reverend John Bodycomb, who was responsible for the survey, made the following trenchant comments:

> It's an assault on people to bore them. Really to bore other people is almost an act of symbolic violence against them, but to bore people in God's name, boy, that's something really serious. I think that's blasphemous to stand up and say 'Thus sayeth the Lord', and then bore people rigid. I don't think there's any excuse for that.[27]

No, there isn't. Preachers are not, of course, in the business of entertaining but, while congregations might pick up something from the atmosphere of a worship service by osmosis, they will not acquire biblical

---

26. See http://www.columbia.edu/~jh299/DA.html. The role and importance of 'the dopamine factor' in human behaviour is disputed among interpretation theorists. It is still speculative work.
27. 'Religion Report', ABC Radio, Australia, Wednesday 8 July 2004. http://www.abc.net.au/rn/talks/8.30/relrpt/trr9828.htm

knowledge that way. Biblical knowledge does have to be taught but this 'pulpit teaching' must use the tools of effective communication. Without those tools the preacher's task is compromised: passion is subverted by doctrine; the glowing life of the bible is reduced to dry bones and dust by well-meant but counterproductive literalism; and the preacher's pulpit is converted into a teacher's lectern. 'Preachers,' our hearers ask, 'can these bones live?'[28] Among the tools preachers need to call to their aid are the techniques of the entertainer—sound presentational structure, carefully crafted and even lyrical language, dramatic sensibilities, and emotional balance that is neither sentimental nor manipulative—provided the means adopted serve the message rather than overpowering it. The Right Reverend Paul Moore, Jr, sometime Bishop of New York, held strong views on this point that are worth noting:

> Some of our clergy read their sermons. It drives me wild. Preaching is not teaching, it's not lecturing. It's preaching. I think you should communicate as much as possible with your whole being. It's more like acting. And if you get Laurence Olivier up there banging it out, it's something else.[29]

I don't think Bishop Moore was necessarily arguing against preaching from written texts; most people do better with a text. He is talking about preaching *effectively*. Effective communication from a text means, in part, learning the art of looking as if one is not reading. It is not a difficult skill and its lack in preachers drives our four lay respondents as wild as it did the bishop. Reading

---

28 . Ezekiel 27:2.

29. *New York Times*, 14 January 1998, quoted in Thornton & Washburn, *op cit* (note 20 above), 3.

sermons was roundly condemned along with a range of other technical 'crimes' such as poor handling of papers, poor use of microphones, poor projection and poor enunciation.

Effective communication is also enhanced by another factor stressed in various ways by all four respondents. They are looking for signs from preachers of 'connectedness'. 'Who are you and what do you have to say that's relevant to me? Why should I listen to you?'[30] asked the young woman whose father is an Anglican priest. She went on to say with passion and exasperation:

> Preachers have often had so much to say to me in so far as how I should live or what I should be doing and how I should follow Christ while at the same time they don't seem to be communicating at a particularly high level of emotional [or] self-awareness. There is a certain piety about this that drives me insane.[31]

She concluded in words that ought to make all of us who preach check out our social lives and our diaries:

> I want to see the evidence of your connectedness with both yourself and the world around you. Spread yourselves out into the world. Expand your horizons. Go to the movies. Talk to people. Anyone about anything. Don't preach yet. Just listen. Get in touch. I think good preaching comes from this

30. Ruth Pickard, unpublished paper 'Don't Call Me a Postmodernist but . . .', St Mark's National Theological Centre, Canberra, 2 April 2004, 2.
31. *Ibid*, 5.

> kind of personal ground work and this kind of cultural homework.[32]

Perhaps the most sobering comments, and those that cannot be passed over by anyone who wants to claim the title 'evangelist', fall in the 'don't waste my time' category. It was pointed out that, no matter what other things a preacher might do during his or her week, no matter what the demands of pastoral ministry might be (and they were respectfully acknowledged to be heavy), when it comes to evangelistic opportunities with 'outsiders', our time in the pulpit is vital and, indeed, probably the only chance we are going to get.

> Why it matters is quite simple: for the outsiders like me, who would otherwise never experience the pastoral side, this is our first actual point of contact with the Church. When *you* step into the pulpit, you are *it*. You have fifteen minutes in which to establish your legitimacy, both your own, that of the Church, and of the God whom you serve.[33]

Fifteen minutes: it is this inescapable immediacy which confronts preachers with the question, 'how am I different from anyone else who gives a public address?' The answer is both simple and terrifying. It is quite simply that preachers must believe in the *absolute truth* at the heart of what they say. It is entirely possible for a public speaker, academic, politician, public servant, or lawyer to have reservations about the validity of their material, even to believe something quite other than what they say, but it is not possible for one to preach the Christian gospel without believing that *God is*. Not, that is, if they are to

---

32. *Ibid*, 9.
33. Cheung, *op cit*, 10.

invest their material with authenticity and show evidence of personal integrity and genuine authority. For preachers, 'connectedness', and the wrestling with paradox and the great questions of living to which I referred above, are about the fundamental question: What is truth?

Which question brings us to an uncomfortable but inescapable reality. Preachers, like those to whom we preach, are forever held between two poles. On the one hand, we are all creatures of God and known by God. *O Lord, you have searched me out and known me . . . where can I go from your spirit? Or where can I flee from your presence?* sang the psalmist.[34] Anglicans encounter that same sense of God-as-Other in the great and confronting prayer with which we begin every eucharist: 'Almighty God, to whom all hearts are open, all desires known, and from whom no secrets are hidden; cleanse the thoughts of our hearts by the inspiration of your Holy Spirit, that we may perfectly love you, and worthily magnify your holy name'. On the other hand, we are called, in words from the great Shema, to love this God from whom there is no hiding, who grants no privacy: *'you shall love the Lord your God with all your heart, and with all your soul, and with all your mind, and with all our strength . . . Beware, lest your heart be deceived, and you turn and serve other gods, and worship them . . . I am the Lord, your God.*[35] Quite simply, we cannot magnify God's holy name unless we believe that that name is the answer to the question, what is truth? Our respondents are asking us to stand in the pulpit and say that—'I believe'—but also to say 'Lord, help my unbelief'. They are saying to us 'believe in the things of which you speak, but believe in yourselves as creatures of God, just as we

34. Psalm 139:1, 7.
35. Selected verses from the *Shema*, http://www.jewfaq.org/prayer/shema.htm

are; show us that you too are vulnerable and full of doubt and speak of that which is real and true and of your life and ours, and whisper to us of God's view of what should be'.

Well might we whisper. Neither preachers nor those to whom we preach are separate from God and yet God is as separate from us as earth from sky. To preachers falls the lot to tell of the mystery of that divide. It is an impossible task but so be it—remember Morris West's fool preaching to a heedless world? We are called to witness to both division and the seamless garment. With the whole people of God we say 'we believe in one God, the Father, the Almighty, maker of heaven and earth'[36] and yet we also say that 'for us and for our salvation' this almighty God 'became truly human'. *Credo,* our ancestors sang, and, in our turn, we declare 'we believe'. The challenge is to find the metaphors, images, symbols and simple words that will make the connections for us—and for our hearers—between God-with-us and God, Lord and Judge of all, as well as between Bible and world. I am reminded of an incident in my childhood that has become very real to me in my life as a preacher. I was in Sydney with my family and on a Manly ferry docking at Circular Quay. I remember seeing a woman, obviously in a hurry and too impatient to wait for the gangplank, rush to the opening in the ferry's rail and step out for the wharf. At that exact moment, the ferry hove to and she was left stretching further and further to touch the wharf. She's still there in my mind suspended over the water churning between ferry and wharf along with the questions of my child's mind: Will she make it? Will she split in two? Will she fall into the water and be crushed or drowned?

That memory symbolises for me the preacher's dilemma. We stand stretched out, between the solid

---

36. The Nicene Creed, *A Prayer Book for Australia* (Sydney: Broughton Books, 1995), 123.

ground of the Bible, our foundational text, and the far less certain and less stable context of the world in which we live. And it's our task to stay there between them, reaching out and touching both, creating a bridge. It is a dangerous place to be. How can we not be torn in two? On the one hand, in the world we encounter politics, money, power, violence and carnage, and news, news, news—often more than we can handle. On the other hand, in the Bible we encounter politics, money, power, violence and carnage, good news and Easter.[37] The chasm between these two worlds can seem very large, and just as dangerous as those churning waters. Our modern world of plumbed water and sewerage, of telephones, aeroplanes and the internet is distant by more than simply time from the biblical world where most people travelled only as far as they could walk. Nevertheless, for all the vast differences, it sometimes seems that Ecclesiastes was right, and there is nothing new under the sun,[38] that ancient stories are played out again and again with only a change of clothing to tell them apart. Think of war, any war, and time dissolves in the blood and guts of killing.

The preacher's dilemma can neither be denied nor relativised and we are not done with its challenges yet. As preachers we may well stand between Bible and world and touch them both with our words but we too are of the world. We are not somehow different from, or better than, or less sinful than, or more godly than, anyone else. We are both part of the problem that is living and beneficiaries of the solution that we preach, the Good News of Jesus Christ. This is a reality we dare not forget. Nor dare we forget that God is already present with, and active

37. The idea for this comparison came from the Foreword of William H Willimon to Fleming Rutledge, *The Bible and the New York Times* (Grand Rapids: Eerdmans, 1998), xiii.

38. Ecclesiastes 1:9.

among, those to whom we preach. In this context, Garrison Keillor's words stand as a salutary warning:

> When a minister stands in front of people he is interrupting what the people have come to church for. He had better have a good reason for doing that . . . We go [to church] to look at the mysteries, and all the substitutes for communion with God are not worth anyone's time.[39]

All four respondents mentioned the question of integrity and honesty in preaching. Laziness and 'faking it' are easy to spot, we were told, infuriating and inexcusable. They are betrayals of the preacher's task and signs of 'parsimoniousness . . . miser-liness of spirit and basic contempt for the congregation'.[40] There was no mistaking the anger from all our respondents about being subjected to shoddy preaching. 'Complacency is treason for preachers', said one, and continued:

> I often go to services for the music, but if it turns out to be an ordinary choir . . . then I shrug—it's not a concert, after all . . . But if the sermon is a desultory compilation of 'thoughts for the day' apparently copied from somebody's desk calendar, and the liturgy appears to be an experiment in chaos theory, then I really start to wonder . . . surely the sermon and the liturgy must form part of your fundamental duty of care. If you can't be bothered working on that, then perhaps you ought

39. Garrison Keillor, quoted in Charles L Rice, *The Embodied Word* (Minneapolis: Fortress Press, 1989), 51.
40. Cheung, *op cit,* 11.

> seriously to reconsider the nature of your vocation.[41]

Once a preacher's vocation is questioned we have reached the soft underbelly of the preacher's life. No *apologia* will convince. Vocation can only be evidenced by fulfilling the preacher's task as ordained. Underpinning this, and the respondents' complaints to us at St Mark's, is the demand that preachers demonstrate, not only hard work, but self-knowledge, humility and vulnerability. The clear call is for incarnational preaching. The two great vices for preachers are arrogance and fear and they are death to incarnational preaching. The two great virtues are humility and vulnerability, and without these two virtues incarnational preaching will not occur. They are the compost and the water needed to feed the ground from which incarnational sermons will grow.

Humility and vulnerability are difficult to grasp for anyone, not least for preachers. If we are any good, we face the danger of arrogance and pride. We can forget that the word we preach must be God's and not ours. Self-aggrandisement is just one of a bunch of sinful characters who crowd into pulpits with preachers and will wrest the Word of God from them if given half a chance. On the other hand, if we suspect we're not so good, we can strangle the Word of God with fear and insecurity. We can retreat into dictatorial and moralistic demands that our hearers see things the way we do or be damned to hell. Arrogance and fear both lead to bombast, not to preaching the Word of God.

Preaching needs to be grounded, in the Bible and in prayer, certainly, but no less in humility and that is something we human beings find hard to remember, no matter what we say. We can never remind ourselves too

41. Cheung, *loc cit.*

often that we are not God and the best we can do is struggle to catch a glimpse of God and try to explain what that might be like. To bring our hearers to recognise God in their own lives, not because of the power of our words but through the power of God's grace which sometimes—if we're lucky—might use us as vehicles. Unless we expose ourselves, our struggles and our doubts, and show that we are as vulnerable as the next person to hurt, pain and suffering, we will sustain no one. We will comfort no one. We will inspire no one. And the grace of God will be neither known by us nor glimpsed through us.

Isaiah's words quoted at the beginning call us to *walk in the flame of [y]our fire,* which means we are to be grounded in our own lives, to know who we are, what swords stick in our sides and what dark secrets we hide within us. We are called, therefore, to accept vulnerability and risk. Isaiah calls us to *walk . . . among the brands that [we] have kindled,* which means we are to be grounded in community with people with whom we share the journey to God. We are called, therefore, to show ourselves as one with them in belief and unbelief. Isaiah calls us to *walk in darkness and [have] no light, yet trus[t] in the name of the Lord and [rely] upon . . . God,* which means we are to be grounded in Scripture and the spiritual life. We are called, therefore, to be holy and to lead others to mature Christian holiness.

Remember the story of Jesus doodling with his finger on the ground?[42] A woman had been brought to him and was in danger of being stoned for adultery. Jesus twice *wrote with his finger on the ground.* Buying time to think? Emphasising the point he wanted to make? Doodling as he listened to her tell her story? We, too, have a story to tell—the story of the Christ who drew a line in the dust—and the line *we* draw in the sand says *et homo factus*

42. John 8:6–8.

est . . . credo. God is. God speaks. God became truly human. This we believe. On that line preachers must stand, nose to nose with the world, as it were, telling the story, striving and disputing earnestly but respectfully, listening not condemning, enticing not dictating, in the hope that some to whom they speak might also say *credo . . .* I believe.

The point of hope for the future for all of us who preach is that, despite the often swingeing criticisms that were made by our lay respondents at St Mark's, they are willing to come and listen, even if for some it is only occasionally. There is for them an as yet unquenched hope that some day, somewhere, the grace of God might flash out of the words from the pulpit, that human words might suddenly become the Word and, even if only for a moment, 'what is truth?' is answered. The insight and inspiration of that moment may not necessarily be joyful. It may indeed be a reaffirmation of the existence of pain, but it will be of a pain shared, a struggle belonging to all. It is the task of preachers, as *kindlers of fire* and *lighters of firebrands*, to keep that hope alive.

3
Lanterns at Dusk? Preaching After Modernity

Bruce Barber

The preaching of the gospel today in Western society is in danger of taking on the character of prattle, in that the preached word no longer proceeds out of the reality to which it is supposed to give expression.[1]

Establishing the context

The title plays on the imagery of Friedrich Nietzsche's Parable of the Madman from *The Gay Science* of 1887. In the parable, the madman, in his unsuccessful search for God, lights a puny little lantern at noon, that is, at the time of the emancipated world's maximum illumination. One can hardly imagine a better image of the fate of God in a world which has come to regard itself as having achieved its majority, of having 'come of age'. If the parable is accurate, and God has indeed become unlocateable in the world for the first time in history, it follows that Christian faith will inevitably find itself in a perilous situation. Such a conclusion needs little contemporary demonstration.

'Modern' theology, that is theology pursued in the afternoon, had no option but to deal with this radically new situation. Consequently, it set itself the task of reconstruction from 'the ground up', a spatial metaphor itself of some significance. It rightly took this emerging

1. Robert Funk, *Language, Hermeneutic, and Word of God* (New York: Harper and Row, 1966), 9.

world with great seriousness, aware that after 'the Death of God' it would have to construct a new foundational 'religious *a priori*'. Accordingly, the nineteenth century is witness to a relentless search for appropriate anthropological foundations which could be proposed as capable of bearing the weight of a new theological enterprise.

After two hundred years of experiment in this regard, it is perhaps not premature to conclude that the success of modern theology has been at best problematic. Insofar as preaching has largely conformed itself to the paradigms proposed by a variety of such theologies, the consequences for preaching also are correspondingly monumental. For if the pathos of 'modern', that is to say, post-Enlightenment theology, is that it 'always arrives too late', how much more must the 'modern' sermon suffer the same anachronistic fate.

The power of the parable, therefore, both in its contemporaneity and in its shaping of this paper, warrants reproduction in its entirety:

> Have you not heard of the madman who lit a lantern at noonday, ran to the market-place, and cried unceasingly, 'I am looking for God! I am looking for God!' Since it happened that there were many standing there who did not believe in God, he roused great laughter. Is he lost? said one. Or gone astray like a child?, said another. Or has he hidden himself? Is he afraid of us? Has he gone on a voyage? Or emigrated? So they shouted and laughed. The madman leapt into their midst, and pierced them with his glance. 'Where has God gone?' he cried. 'I will tell you. We have slain him—you and I. We are all his murderers. But how did we do it?

How could we drink up the sea? Who gave us the sponge to wipe out the whole horizon? What did we do, when we unchained this earth from its sun? Where is it moving to now? And where are we moving to now? Away from all suns? Do we not stumble all the time? Backwards, sideways, forwards, in every direction? Is there an above and a below any more? Are we not wandering as through infinite nothingness? Does empty space not breathe upon us? Is it not colder now? Is not night coming and evermore night? Must we not light lanterns at noon? Do we not hear the noise of the grave-diggers, as they bury God? Do we not smell God decaying? —Gods too decay! God is dead. God stays dead. And we have slain him. How shall we console our-selves, chief of all murderers? The holiest and most powerful that the world has ever possessed has ebbed its blood away beneath our knives—who will wipe this blood from our fingers? What water can make us clean? What sacred rites will we have to invent? Is not the greatness of this deed too great for us? Must we not ourselves become gods, in order to seem worthy of them? There was never a greater deed, and because of it all who are born after us are part of a higher history than ever was before!'

The madman fell silent, and looked at his hearers again. They too were silent, and looked at him with shocked eyes. At last he threw his lantern on the ground, so that it broke in pieces, and went out. 'I come too

> early,' he said, 'it is not yet my time. This monstrous event is still on the way—it has not yet penetrated men's ears. Lightening and thunder needs time, the light of the stars need time, deeds need time, even after they have been done, in order to be seen and heard. This deed is still further from men than the remotest stars—and yet they have done it.'
>
> The story goes that the madman went into several churches on the same day and sang his requiem to the eternal God. Led out and questioned, he replied just the one thing: 'What are the churches, if not the tombs and sepulchres of God?'[2]

At least one dimension of the pathos of this parable is that the people in the market place—'the herd' to adopt Nietzsche's contemptuous description—are ignorant of this epochal revolution which is in the process of taking place. (Let the reader beware!) Only the *cognoscente*, in the person of the *Übermensch* (the Overman), of whom Nietzsche himself is the progenitor, understands its radicality.

What follows, therefore, is an attempt to provide a theological commentary on this parable relative to the task of preaching today.

2. Friedrich Nietzsche, *Fröhliche Wisenschaft* 125 [as translated in Gerhard Ebeling, *The Nature of Faith* (Philadelphia: Fortress Press, Philadelphia 1961), 77–78].

The question to the market place: where is God?

Nietzsche's critique cannot simply be dismissed, much less avoided, because it strikes too near the core of Christian faith[3]

It has become something of a truism to assert that preaching today in mainstream denominations in the West is in a state of crisis. This observation is confirmed at many levels, not least by consulting a dictionary entry under 'preaching'. Dictionaries, of course, are seldom helpful for theological investigation, as any teacher who has had responsibility for reading first year theological assignments can testify. But in this matter, consultation of a dictionary is a depressing, albeit a salutary, place to start. Thus Webster's third New International Dictionary describes a sermon as 'an annoying harangue', and the act of preaching as: 'to exhort in an officious or tiresome manner'—hardly a promising place to begin a potential rehabilitation of the sermon. Then, too, from within the theological circle we might recall that, in a book now forty years old, 'The Trouble with the Church', Helmut Thielicke employed a revealing, if disconcerting, image of the church building as a large crying room—a designated area for infants popular in newly constructed churches in the 1960's, but now extended to comprise the whole of the worship space. Between preacher and congregation, he suggested, is interposed a thick glass wall. Preacher and hearer can see each other, but there is no sound—only moving lips and bodily gestures witnessed by those who have now become not so much hearers as 'spectators'. Something more sinister is clearly at stake here than the lament of the writer of Ecclesiastes: 'All words wear

3. David Bentley Hart, *The Beauty of the Infinite* (Grand Rapids: Eerdmans, 2004), 94.

themselves out, more than one can express. The eye is not satisfied with seeing, nor the ear filled with hearing' (1:8).

These negativities undoubtedly have their genesis in historical human experience, although this has not always been the case. The story is told of an eighteenth century Scottish divine who had been preaching for almost an hour, but on giving signs that he was coming to a close, the congregation as one body rose, crying: 'For God's sake, go on, go on'. These, it is clear, were the good old days, especially for preachers.

From such a high experience for both preacher and hearers, what is responsible for the sermon's comparatively recent collapse? The conventional wisdom states that the latter half of the twentieth century inaugurated the shift from an aural to a visual culture. In this connection, while it might have been helpful for Luther to have enjoined in the sixteenth century: 'Stick your eyes in your ears', this injunction is hardly likely to solve the problem as it presents itself to us, useful though this advice continues to be. Notwithstanding the validity of the cultural claim, the burden of this paper is to propose that at a more fundamental level, the modern crisis for preaching is attributable to anachronistic, if not questionable, theologies undergirding the present form and content of the representative sermon.

In this regard, it is useful to rehearse what might be termed the theological maelstrom of the second half of the twentieth century in the English speaking world. Preachers of mature years have lived through a succession of theological 'crises', as each was somewhat self-importantly designated, which in turn had their differing impacts on the construction, not to speak of the actual viability, of the sermon. Protestant preachers who, in their youth, were nurtured in the ecclesially vaguely labelled contest between 'liberalism' and 'conservatism', were likely to have been theologically formed in what (polemically) has sometimes latterly been designated as 'neo-Orthodox quasi-Platonic speculative trinitarianism'. This foundation was soon, in quick succession, to be undermined by a rapid procession of possibilities. In some cases most of the 'new theologies' were enthusiastically, even if temporarily, welcomed. To list but some of the theological options available over the last forty years: the death of God theology, secular theology, the new mysticism, liberation theology, process theology, feminist theology, post-liberal theology, post-foundational theology. Consequently, it would be no exaggeration to claim that, at its most extreme, the magnitude of the crisis for preaching today arises from the critical question of whether inherited theological conceptualities can be the vehicle for the kerygma at all.

If this is at all true, then the problem for preaching is not so much that of the relationship between exegesis and other disciplines of theology, as most of the homiletical books suppose, but is rather that of the unity and coherence of the gospel itself in a world that is radically different from that which is received and explored in these disciplines. If the problem is as fundamental as this, then it follows that the recovery of preaching today must inevitably be something in the nature of an experiment —this not in the first instance to be understood as replacing preaching's external traditional form with a new model of communication, as is frequently advocated, so much as an experiment in repristinating preaching's internal content.

Two specific problems might be identified at the outset. First, if it is rare to find in the books about preaching an identification of critical theological presuppositions of the sermon, it is even rarer to discover much of a larger analysis of the cultural forces which have been at work in Western society contributing to preaching's malaise. For the fact is that where substantial theological cultural analysis is lacking, homiletical considerations are likely to be 'docetic', that is, they are situated 'beyond' contemporary prevailing contextual realities, with all their scarcely visible complexities.

Second, exacerbating this external nature of the crisis and the many suggested alternatives to the traditional sermon, must also be identified the internal crisis of the actual isolation—if not the practical silence—of the theological disciplines from the preaching task. This can be observed at the popular level of the sermon books designed to help the preacher, but not only there. Even where these inherited disciplines are in practice identified, it is not uncommon to polarise the issues around hoary dichotomies such as those of theory and practice, past and present, content and form. Inevitably within such a framework, 'theology', to use the word generically, is understood to be the concern of the first of these dualities, homiletics the second.

This bifurcation of the issues on the one hand effectively insulates theology from really impinging on the preaching task, and, on the other, leaves the preacher without any concrete guidance as to how a sermon might take shape in a particular community. In any case, and as a matter of fact, the actual experience of preachers in constructing a sermon testifies to the fact that 'what to say' and 'how to say it' are not so easily distinguished.

What is the structure of Christian preaching? It is clearly important to ask this question at the outset, not necessarily in order immediately to provide a satisfying or final definition, but rather to test where the issues are seen to lie. An answer to this question will be the fundamental concern of the next section. For now, it is sufficient to observe that if one looks at the phenomenon of preaching, and the participants and ingredients in the enterprise, two obvious elements are present. There are people involved—preacher and congregation—and there is a book of texts. It is understandable that an initial attempt at answering the question: 'What is a sermon?', while attempting to hold all the ingredients together, will likely privilege one or the other of these two elements. If the former is the emphasis, the 'problem' of the sermon will be seen to be one of communication; if the latter, the weight will fall on the difficulties of exegesis, namely how to overcome the 'pastness' of the texts, since the texts clearly come from an 'other' world that is long gone. The popularity in our day of the phrase 'where people are at' indicates that the not inconsiderable problem of communication is likely, in fact, to take centre stage to the eclipse of the more fundamental issue of what it is that is ingredient in our homiletical endeavours.

In former times, the decision to understand the sermon by giving priority either to 'people' or 'texts' may not have carried particularly fateful consequences, since there appeared to be a homogeneity of expectation both ecclesiastically and culturally in contexts explicitly understanding themselves to be Christian, as the eighteenth century illustration above evidences. It would be possible, however, to assert that the oft quoted nineteenth century —quintessentially modern—definition of the sermon by Phillips Brooks, the most considerable American preacher of his generation, succinctly states one dimension of the contemporary problem. He proposed that preaching is 'Truth mediated through a personality', a formulation that appealed to something that was both a reflection, as well as the source, of a certain style of preaching. This style inevitably focussed on technique and the performance of the preacher. The consequences of this understanding of preaching can still—though with diminishing frequency—be observed by consulting the often contrived sermon titles appearing on Protestant church notice boards, not to speak of the practice, for the preaching of the sermon, of dimming the lights over the nave while the pulpit orator is suffused in light.

If one turns primarily to the other pole for an understanding of preaching, namely the Bible and its plethora of texts offered Sunday by Sunday, problems of a different kind emerge. The impression might then be given that, so far as preaching is concerned, the primary reality is: 'In the beginning was the text'. This necessity to be 'faithful to the text' is likely to suffer from a foreshortened vision, if it is forgotten that the text is already in the service of something beyond itself, namely the gospel—that reality which occasioned the particular text in the first place.

So much for these introductory comments. Already presupposed, but not explicitly identified, are three crucial *theological* decisions which, either implicitly or explicitly, influence the way we understand preaching. They may be put as three questions: (i) what is the *gospel* (the dogmatic question); (ii) what is the Bible (the exegetical question); and (iii) who is the contemporary hearer (the situational question). We start with the third of these questions.

Who is the contemporary hearer? Christian faith's cultural crisis

Have you not heard of the madman who lit a lantern at noonday, ran to the market-place, and cried unceasingly: "I am looking for God! I am looking for God!" Since there were many standing there who did not believe in God, he roused great laughter . . .

So begins this arresting and unrelenting disclosure of Western culture's theological crisis, noting that now almost one hundred and twenty years have passed since Nietzsche could rejoice that the sun of the Enlightenment was at its zenith—hence the pathos of the madman lighting his puny theological lantern in his quest for God.

What did Nietzsche intend by this theological announcement of the death of God, which is the burden of the parable? The parable itself suggests an answer: '*We have slain him. How shall we console ourselves, chief of all murderers? . . . Is not the greatness of this deed too great for us? Must we not ourselves become gods . . .?*'

What would it mean for human beings to kill God, and thus become gods themselves? It surely means this: the achievement of the Enlightenment aimed at bringing about a fundamental 'turn to the human subject' as the signifier of a new reality called modernity. To comprehend the significance of this turn, it is necessary to understand the previous medieval world view from which modernity represented such a departure. For if at the highpoint of the medieval structure of reality, *God* occupied the apex as the *ens realissimum,* the most real being on which all else rested, then, within the space of three hundred years, this most radical theistic overturning of Western culture had been achieved. One can doubt everything, claimed Descartes—modernity's first philosopher—but what cannot be doubted is the reality of the self doubting. Hence the notorious *cogito ergo sum:* I think, therefore I am.

To be sure, the noonday sun has continued to burn ever brighter in so much of modern culture that it ill behooves us who are modernity's substantial beneficiaries to be disdainful of its rays. To speak only of one legacy of modernity, many already have been—and it is certain that many more will in the future find themselves to be—the recipients of a medical technology which makes life both quantitatively and qualitatively more sustainable. We might, however, hazard whether television screens on refrigerator doors offer similar significance, not to speak of the increasingly more effete legacies of modern technology.

However bright modernity's world may be found to be, even with its acknowledged and indisputable accompanying shadows, it is not here that one wants to speak of approaching gloom. Rather it is in its theological and a/theological musings in which—to continue the imagery of the parable—'one experiences *'the breathings of empty space'*, of the *'coming of a night and ever more night'*, and of the increasingly frenetic lighting of lanterns by a culture destined to live out its life after the madman's discovery of 'the death' of God.

Although a deity of a sort was required by the philosopher/mathematician Descartes to complete the system—he was after all a regular attender at Mass—the fundamental anthropocentric premise was from this point on securely in place. It did not take long for the consolidation of this innovation to emerge. If Descartes had established the human self as the epistemological subject, it was not such a large step to the even more significant Immanuel Kant—a weighty Christian name surely!—who postulated the self as a free and responsible actor, and who is largely responsible for the fateful reduction of the subject matter of theology to morality, and of the conversion of the gospel into its contemporary moralistic self-justifying straightjacket. Thus the funeral eulogy: 'He'—it is almost always a 'he'—'was a real Christian; he did not go to church, but he lived a truly good life'. We ought not to be surprised that there remained only another very short step after Kant, which Friedrich Nietzsche was pleased to take, namely that of demanding the self to assume itself to be the source of all knowledge. And since there cannot be two sources of authority, the death of the theistic God of Western culture consequently becomes inevitable. Thus the individual subject, mind or spirit now becomes primary, and takes over the initiative and functions which had once been the prerogatives of deity.

It is important to register that Nietzsche's conclusion of the death of God came after at least a century of theology attempting to accommodate itself to the new anthropocentric world that had brought to an end the long-standing theological grounding of Christendom. In this respect, Nietzsche's significance lies in the fact that he was the first to diagnose modernity as nihilism, which the death of God inaugurated. For our purposes, however, his greater significance rests in his insistence that modernity is simply the final phase of the disease called Christianity: witness the scarifying judgment of the madman in his devastating conclusion: 'What are the churches but the tombs and sepulchres of God?' Consequently, however successful nineteenth century churches might have judged the 'new' theologies to be for the articulation of Christian faith, what is decisive is their crushing failure, if Nietzsche can be taken as an illustration of the 'cultured despiser'—Schleiermacher's putative interlocutor—on whose behalf that modern project was undertaken.

That theology was so affected by this anthropocentric turn is indisputable. For anthropocentric modern theology, accommodating itself to the prevailing culture, determined to begin—as indeed it continues—with an understanding of God conceived apart from Christ and the Spirit, as any hospital chaplain is compelled to acknowledge in the sometimes frustrating pastoral encounter with a terminal cancer patient. Protesting existential disenchantment with an erstwhile, and now confirmed, impotent modern 'unbaptised God' (Robert Jenson), patient depression or anger lie not far below the surface. In personally less confronting guises, but with equally disastrous consequences, this onto-theological God was the subject of the relentless quests of nineteenth century theology for an appropriate anthropocentric theological foundation for the articulation of Christian faith. The onto-theological God is that deity which is a construct of the Western philosophical theological tradition, and is the God of that Christianity which Nietzsche called 'Platonism for the masses'. For our purposes, then, if it be true that there is a close correlation between theology and preaching, we ought not to be surprised that the public preaching presided over by modernity's apologetic theologies is no less affected by this methodological starting point.

In a word, the fundamental problem for modern, that is Enlightenment driven, theology was, and is, to establish its relevance in and to an increasingly skeptical world. It thus requires what might be called 'a world verification' principle. The consequential question for preaching in the modern world was, and is, not so much the matter of the truth of the Christian gospel, as it is its 'relevance'—its meaning and its credibility given the required new starting point. After at least two hundred years of this way of proceeding, it is not premature to conclude that the essential outcome both for modern world verification theology, and its counterpart in modern apologetic preaching, is that both always arrive 'too late', since they are theology and preaching in defensive mode. Such preaching asks first of all: how does 'modern man' —interpreting this anachronistic phrase in its inclusive sense—understand reality? Once that question has apparently been satisfactorily answered, the resulting category discovery—the anthropocentric 'religious *a priori*' —becomes the foundation for the articulation of the gospel. But if the world already understands the primacy of that foundation, of what further revelatory significance is the gospel? That is the pathos of modern theology unveiled with piercing clarity by Nietzsche's madman.

It is salutary to observe that, notwithstanding the monumental theological achievements of the great

European Protestant theologians of the twentieth century in their rediscovery of what they came to see as being a more proper theological agenda than that pursued by their immediate forebears, there has been very little subsequent impact on the understanding of the gospel—much less its enthusiastic reception—in their churches (in Australia at least). These theologians did their work amidst the crashing of falling masonry as the old Enlightenment theological foundations crumbled around them, in order to speak a new word from God to those wandering dazedly amongst the ruins. One thinks of such figures as the Swiss Karl Barth and Emil Brunner; of the German Paul Tillich, Friedrich Gogarten and Dietrich Bonhoeffer; or of the Dutch, Kornelis Miskotte and Hans Hoekendijk. Despite their significant and sometimes monumental achievements, the old apologetic of presumed cultural 'relevance' continues its dominance, even if in more and more epiphenomenal forms.

Two hundred years of preaching constructed on this model makes it difficult to imagine that there might be another way. Whether designated modern or post-modern, it is indisputable that there is a contemporary crisis both for Christian theology and Christian proclamation. These two enterprises, for good or ill, go hand in hand. The negative thesis of this paper is that modern preaching, so characteristic of most liberal Western churches, is anachronistic, in the sense that the cultural presuppositions of modernity have rapidly become unsustainable as a foundation for the proclamation of the gospel. The positive thesis is the proposal that the time is ripe for a constructive post-liberal theology and preaching, which, unlike that offered by a defensive modern liberal theology, is able to take the offensive in a climate of radical cultural disintegration. The real problem, however, is that a self-labeling liberal Christian—not to speak of her fundamentalist *alter ego*

—appears to be the last cultural enthusiast for modernity, being blissfully unaware that the old apologetic game is over.

Lex praedicandi, lex credendi: so we preach and so we believe: the gospel and the Bible

What would it mean if, instead of trying to explain the gospel in terms of our scientific culture, we tried to explain our culture in terms of the gospel?[4]

A previous section of this paper offered three foundational questions basic to a consideration of preaching, and suggested that their ordering was of equal significance. Fragmentary though it has been, sufficient for our purposes, has possibly been said in answer to the question: who is the contemporary hearer?

Of the other two questions, 'what is the gospel', and 'what is the Bible', their ordering is of paramount significance in pursuing the claim for a more creative outcome for preaching. Why is the order of the questions significant? Most structured theological education has chronologically privileged the Bible over theology. Church documents invariably preface their concerns with the formula: 'The biblical and theological basis for . . . ' All that needs to be said to this is: the Church had a faith before it had a text since the Bible itself is a theological text. Not least the urgency of the rehabilitation of preaching today consists in repudiating, not the content, but the ordering of this formula, as the proposed answers to the questions to come will suggest. But before proceeding with this agenda, it is more than time to

4. Leslie Newbiggin, *Foolishness to the Greeks* (Geneva: WCC Mission Series, 1986), 41

propose a definition of the sort of preaching which is being advocated.

A provisional definition would go something like this: *preaching is that event in which the biblical text comes to expression as the concrete manifestation of the hearers' identity.*

The key terms are 'event', 'coming to expression', and 'hearers' identity'. Scarcely concealed in this definition is the close correlation between the event that is the *past* hearing of a text and its present hearing. This inclusive correlation always embodies not only the exegesis of texts, but also incorporates the wider consciousness of church history—both its cultural engagement and its pastoral tradition—and its theological legacies in the form of past as well as present doctrinal formulations. And all this with the aim of instantiating a new human identity as a social phenomenon called 'church', since the hearer in this under-standing is always a plural identity, not a singular.

With the above as a working definition, we turn to the first of the remaining two questions.

What is the gospel, or 'where is reality to be found?'

The fundamental question here shows itself to be: what constitutes reality. It has already been suggested that the history of theology illustrates the way in which this question has been culturally answered, that is, whether in the final analysis, the world is to be explained by God, as is the case in pre-modernity—sometimes called 'revelation' verification where the key term is that of the world's intended corresponding 'identity' with that of its Creator and Redeemer, or whether on the other hand, as in modernity, God is to be explained by the world—'world' verification with its associated key term of 'relevance' to the contemporary culture.

In many respects, the history of theology reflects this comparative tension of competing models, although, of course, employing a different conceptual apparatus in each case. It is at base the issue between Tertullian and the Christian Gnostics in the second century; between Anselm in the twelfth and Aquinas in the thirteenth centuries; between Luther and Erasmus in the sixteenth century; between Kierkegaard and Hegel in the nineteenth century; between Barth and Tillich, and Moltmann and liberation theology in the twentieth century. It is, however, of the first importance to observe that the methodological preference for 'God' or the 'world' in constructing theological systems is relatively benign in an essentially theocentric world. The decision as to how to proceed only assumes more than methodological significance in a radically secularised culture such as ours, as is unquestionably demonstrated by Nietzsche's madman after the death of God with his destabilising question: 'what sacred rites will we have to invent?'

With regard to the nature of the sermon in such a world, the matter could perhaps take the form of a question analogous to the theological one posed above: should the sermon be kerygmatic or apologetic, meaning by this distinction, whether it is to be verified by its own subject matter, or by the context in which it is being articulated? The issue, of course, is never so stark or so programmatic, witness Karl Barth's wry observation to the effect that the only true apologetic is the kerygma, because it is addressed to the unbeliever, that is, to the theologian!

If we start with the second formulation which is the presupposition of modernity, preaching is understood to be intentionally and explicitly apologetic. The assumption is that, in varying degrees, God in the gospel functions as the 'unreal', which in preaching has to be shown to be real. Reality here fundamentally belongs to the 'world', but in such a way that, through the skill of the preacher, a compelling way to faith in God might be constructed. But, as has already been suggested, this is precisely the problem of apologetic theology, for in the final analysis, notwithstanding the imaginative and rhetorical skill of the preacher, the 'world' will always prevail, namely, will always 'absorb the newness of the text'.

The alternative to this formulation happens methodologically to be the presupposition of pre-modernity, although it is self-evident that the specific theological content of that epoch is now irretrievably anachronistic. It is significant, however, to note in passing that, within the unified theistic reality of pre-modernity, differing contextual emphases were able to be sustained with relatively benign and inconsequential implications. But the proposal being advocated here is that it is precisely the pre-modern methodological presupposition that is requisite for preaching's engagement with a modern world increasingly experiencing itself as in crisis—a world popularly but imprecisely described as 'post-modern'. That characterisation is imprecise because who knows yet whether such a world is the decadence or the fulfillment of modernity.

The thesis being advocated here is that in late or post-modernity, revelation verification is a much more radical enterprise than in pre-modernity, for, unlike the situation in pre-modernity, it now has to face the impact and challenge of Nietzsche's parable. The point is that preaching in such a world will need to be fundamentally kerygmatic as a diametric counter to the Nietzschean kerygma. That is to say, the gospel is here understood to shatter the everyday, conventional view of what constitutes reality, so that the world, in varying degrees and in its myriad shapes and forms, is revealed to be if not 'unreal' at least 'questionable' in its differing claims to constitute reality. The corollary of this kerygmatic 'deconstruction' is that God may now come to expression in a way which modernity cannot anticipate. What from the world's standpoint is thought of as being vague or shadowy, namely God, is taken in the power of the gospel to be the only reality on which one can rely. In this sense, it will come about as recognition of the fact that it is always theologically the case that the Christian text desires 'to absorb the world' (George Lindbeck), precisely in order to ensure the freedom of the world from all reigning ideologies.

To those still committed to the *modern* theological project, and in defiance of Nietzsche's madman, this project may appear to be a lost cause. We have to take account of the fact that there is a fateful symbiosis of presuppositions at work here. It would be a comparatively simple endeavour if it were the case that the unbaptised onto-theological God of modernity had in fact successfully died. The pathos of the situation disclosed by both Nietzsche's parable and our present experience is that this deity in his/its impotence will not die in the minds of those antagonistic to Christian faith, who think this deity has always been, and must continue to be, the Christian God. The pathos is compounded when modern would-be Christian evangelists reveal that they too hold a good number of the same presuppositions. One has the distinct impression, to limit the conclusion to the demonstrable, that contemporary Protestantism, insofar as it has any appreciation of Nietzsche's concerns at all, desperately hopes that he was wrong, even while secretly suspecting that he may be right. The point is that we are indeed living in approaching twilight, for until the corpse of the onto-theological God of Western culture is satisfactorily interred, the liberating permission given in the gospel to bring its 'baptised God' to new parabolic compelling expression is inhibited. Hence the crisis of our contemporary experiences of preaching.

In any event, regardless of whether preachers have ever understood the issues in these terms, they will almost certainly, tacitly at least, have decided the methodological issue in their own minds. The fundamental question, therefore, is whether preachers are methodologically uncritical, or whether they are methodologically self-conscious theologians with regard to what is at stake. If the question is not an idle one for the self-awareness of the theologian, it is certainly crucial for the theological self-identity of the preacher. It is for this reason that it is of first importance for the preacher to identify something like this crucial presupposition of his or her theology, for on it rests the content and structure of each and every sermon.

Perhaps the matter is most convincingly addressed in the mundane decision concerning sermon illustrations, of which, not surprisingly, preaching manuals in modernity were consistent in their advocacy. The crucial question to be asked however is this: what in our preaching is to be illustrated: the gospel in the light of our experience of the world? or the world in the light of the declaration of the gospel? One may well propose: Ask preachers what they do by way of sermon illustration, and you will discover their theology. Does the preacher illustrate from the world to the gospel or from the gospel to the world? It can virtually be guaranteed that preachers in modernity will have to confirm that the former is their practice. But if by way of rejoinder the response is, as it might well be: 'I do both', then the question will still be pertinent. For now the issue is: how does the actual use of illustrations take shape in the subject matter of the sermon?

What is here being proposed is that the low status and expectations attaching to preaching today lie in this widespread apologetic practice of seeking to illustrate the gospel by life in the world, to which significance is frequently attached the abstract (!) epithet 'reality', or 'the real world'. Not only is this judgment contrary to the claim of the gospel itself—for the 'Lordship of Jesus Christ' must always equate to its latent claim to constitute 'the real' – but its inevitable implication is that the gospel must in varying measure be 'unreal'. If the protest is made—as again is frequently the case—that this appeal to the everyday world is 'how Jesus taught', it becomes important to recognise that the parables, for example, are invariably precisely about what does not happen in the every day world, or if some-thing apparently like that scenario does happen, it does so by way of a radical contrast to that which should happen if we were living in a world redeemed.

The inevitable consequence of world verification preaching is that the sermon has become predictable at best and trite at worst, if not demonstrably unconvincing. Or, as the world both inside and outside the congregation has apparently increasingly decided, 'sermons are boring'. This is not because bright and imaginative material is not being employed, but because the whole venture has become fundamentally predictable, if not pedestrian. As the small auditors in the mercifully now almost universally abandoned Protestant Children's Address in the Sunday service knew only too well, the expected answer to every question put to them by the preacher is always: 'Jesus'!

In the last analysis then, if the world verifies the truth of the gospel, the gospel is merely embroidery on a situation that is in principle known apart from it. Such an assumption obscures the gospel's stated claim to be offering nothing less than the conferral of a new identity. Preaching a gospel of 'relevance' might, of course, still be judged to be 'vital', even 'entertaining', but it will sooner or later show itself to be fundamentally hollow. Why? Because its metho-dological assumption runs counter to the message itself: the world, so it proposes, knows what is real. But is this not that which the gospel seeks to dispute? The consequential implications of the overturning of the conventional practice are many, but we have still to reckon with the third question.

What is the Bible, or, in the sermon, 'who is doing what to whom?'

If the question that underlies the first issue is that of what in the first analysis constitutes reality—the 'naked' world or the enfleshed gospel—the question here is what is to be unfolded by an appeal to biblical texts? Presumably there is, or ought not to be, any dispute that the Bible is central to preaching. But that agreement may conceal divergent understandings which impact negatively on preaching. To put it at its sharpest, is it the preacher's task to explain the text, that is, to regard the text as the means to an end already decided by the preacher, or is it rather the purpose of the text to 'explain' the preacher and, therefore, in the subsequent act of preaching, to 'explain' the hearers. What are the implications of each view? Which is to restate the question 'what does it mean for the Biblical text to come to expression'?

The first view, that it is the preacher's task to explain the text, was, and possibly still is, a statement of universal acceptance, even when in actual practice texts are conspicuous by their absence. At its best, however, the preacher attempts somewhere in the course of the sermon an exegesis to discover what the text meant 'back there' so that it can now be brought over to 'the here and now', exposing its truth in the contemporary world. This, of course, needs to be done, but as a task primarily for the study not the pulpit. Otherwise, the presenting sermon will invariably locate truth in the past and only artificially in the present. How many times have we heard a preacher, having faithfully unfolded the text's contextual complexities, ask, sometimes plaintively but perhaps more often warming at last to the real subject matter: 'Now what has all this to say to us today?' which as hearers is just as likely to lead us to mutter—'not much', perhaps even prefaced by a more colourful adjective.

Where sermons are so constructed, the hearer cannot be blamed for concluding that all significance so far as God is concerned has happened in the past. A consequent characteristic of this model is the overwhelming use of the past tense in preaching: God acted; Jesus Christ died to bring us back to God; the Spirit came. Always the past tense! No wonder that, given the post-modern preoccupations of instantaneity, the overwhelming response to such preaching is boredom. For the fact is that, with rare exceptions, the tense for preaching must always be, if not the future, at least the present.

But what if the statement 'the biblical text comes to expression' means something else? That it is not so much that the text is there to be explained, as it is that the text is there to explain us, that is, to 'expose' us and our situation. With this understanding, creative, even revolutionary, implications are raised for preaching. Consider an illustration. We can propose the analogy of a cat and a mouse. The first view treats the text as the mouse, the preacher being the cat. Cats invariably worry mice. Hence the preacher is seen to worry the text with exegesis, to find out what is really there so that, subsequently, the sermon can apply the appropriate message to the hearers. First there is exegesis, then exposition or application, the aim being to explain the text to a passive hearer.

The second view presents a different picture: the aim here is to allow the text to 'exegete' the preacher, who is always, in the eventfulness of the sermon, the first hearer, but in such a way that there is now set in train a reciprocal dynamic. The text, having found its mark in the preacher/hearer, opens itself to ongoing disclosure to both the preacher as well as the hearer as it reaches its goal. This reciprocal relationship between the text and the hearer constitutes the always surprising, even unexpected, 'aha' for both preacher and hearer. It arises, of course, because the text, which is 'already' preaching becomes so again as something which happens between the preacher and the text, but as a total process involving text, preacher and subsequent hearer in a new reality.

On this understanding, the text is the cat—the 'subject'—while the preacher, the first hearer, and subsequently all hearers together, are, as mice, the 'objects', caught by the text.

A consequence of this understanding is that the preacher will no longer feel the need to illustrate the text with contemporary aids. As has already been suggested, this is a diversionary tactic which defeats the enterprise. For it assumes (i) that the preacher is in control of the text, which is never the case if it be true that the text is always the subject, and it assumes (ii) that the preacher has plumbed the mystery of the text, has it by the throat as it were, the hearers waiting for the preacher to illustrate this mystery by everyday allusions (illusions?) which it is assumed are transparently clear in such a way that they may throw 'light' on the mystery of the text. Such preaching invariably becomes a burden sooner or later to the preacher, as he or she runs out of authentic viable illustrations.

What then of the alternative? The preacher here is rather like a midwife bringing the text to birth such that the text now illustrates the world, which in turn is being disclosed as that which was hitherto opaque. The sermon now is the illustration *par excellence* of what life in the world is intended to be according to Christian truth. That is to say, the sermon, as itself the illustration, means that there is now being offered authentic interpretation, claiming a worldly new reality in place of the predictable old.

There is at least one further consequence. Post-modernity celebrates 'the death of the author'—that is to say, once the text is written, the author has no control over its fate since that control is now in the hands of the hearer. In such a climate, the traditional understanding of the inspiration of Scripture becomes untenable, although its death throes can already be witnessed in modernity. For given its anthropocentric proclivities, modern theology really could do little with the doctrine of the inspiration of Scripture. It functioned there only formally, not materially, in the inconclusive and unconvincing shuttle between respective pneumatological and anthropological claims to past authorship. It thus concentrated on the provenance of the letter of the texts before they occur, rather than pursuing the text's evangelical occurring in the event of preaching. Thus the doctrine of the inspiration of the texts in the modern paradigm is always in danger of remaining simply as an outdated but unusable formulaic relic.

In the turn which this paper is advocating, however, the doctrine of inspiration now becomes central through the recognition that the texts are never ends in themselves, but always are 'inspirited' witnesses to that which comes to them, through them and from them, namely the coming to expression of 'the Word of God'. At least two achievements are secured in such an understanding.

First, the struggle for relevance is in principle concluded. The sermon is truly 'expository' for now the new world of the reign of God has begun to dawn on the predictable scene we call daily life. There is a further bonus. Because the truth has first of all 'exposed' the preacher, preaching, paradoxically, has become somewhat easier and indisputably much more existentially involving than the outmoded paradigm offered by modernity.

Second, the preacher is now out ahead of the world in the way that the gospel is always ahead of the world, since the God who is its creator and redeemer has drawn near. If, as Robert Jenson has so persuasively proposed, in late modernity 'the world has lost its story' because it tried to live a story without a credible storyteller, in contemporary post-modernity—or should that be hyper-modernity—the possibility is that the Church might be the embodiment of that story again, to the end that the world might re-inhabit its proper story.

For the fact is that the test of all preaching is to make the particularities of worldly life transparent to the universality of Christ. Modernity profoundly misunderstood, and continues to misunderstand, this task, seeking as it does to make the particularities of Jesus Christ relevant to a universal world.

Consequently, the time is ripe for the contemporary madman—the preacher—after noonday and with the sun indeed well past its zenith, to light the brightest of lanterns possible to illuminate the impending dusk. For if our lanterns fail at dusk, of what use will they be when the madman's prediction comes true: 'Is not night coming, and ever more night'?

4
The Centrality of Preaching in Christian Worship

Thorwald Lorenzen

Introduction

Worship and preaching are religious phenomena. They are part of the cult practices ('worship' = latin 'cultus') of most major religions. This is especially true for those religions, like Judaism, Islam, Zoroastrianism, Manichaeism, Hinduism and Buddhism, which have a book or books, like the Koran, the Hebrew Bible or Hindu literature, or revealers, like Zarathustra, Mani, or Buddha, as the basis of their faith. They then utilise preaching as the proclamation, interpretation and application of their message. Indeed, within the specific liturgy of a religious worship service, a special sacred language and/or style of delivery can have developed, by which adherents are motivated, challenged and instructed. It is interesting that in these 'word'-centred religions (in contrast to religions in which sacrifices, dramatic cult practices and cult dramas dominate), the word is considered to be more important than the picture. Since people on the whole could not and often cannot, read, they were understood primarily as listeners to and receivers of the word.

The topic of this paper is not worship and preaching in general, but worship and preaching within the Christian context.[1] My questions are related to the identity,

1. There can be no doubt, of course, that since earliest days the Christian communities have adopted and adapted religious elements from their surrounding cultures. Sermons, prayers,

meaning and content of Christian worship. What makes and what keeps Christian worship Christian? My leading concerns are as follows:

a) given that worship and preaching are religious phenomena, I want to inquire as to what is specifically Christian about worship and preaching. By what criterion or criteria do we evaluate our various denominational understandings of preaching in worship? Where are the points of tension and/or conflict between cultural and denominational elements and practices on the one hand, and what we understand to be specifically Christian on the other?

b) what is the place of preaching in Christian worship, and how can we best understand preaching in relation to the other elements that make up Christian worship, especially the 'Lord's supper' (eucharist, holy communion)—and then, of course, the whole of life?

c) to this we add the observation that there seems to be a crisis in preaching today. People in pew and classroom question the importance of preaching. They are bored, they don't want to be told what to do, and they find preaching—often coming down from an exalted pulpit—to be an irrelevant remnant of an authoritarian patriarchal age. Even among serious Christians, one can observe a move away from the 'word' into social action or into liturgical and sacramental renewal.

---

sacred meals and baptisms were known in Judaism, Hellenism and Hellenistic Judaism. But these religio-historical facts raise the theological question in which way they enhance or modify the content of the Christian faith.

These are difficult and controversial issues. Yet, it is not the first time that worship became the centre of controversy in the Christian church. A major reason for the Reformation in the sixteenth century was the nature of the worship service with the eucharistic Mass—understood as a human work and as a sacrifice offered, ever again, to God for the atonement of our sins—at the centre. A clear shift of authority from the church to the Bible and, resulting from that shift, from the eucharist to the word (Martin Luther, Huldrych Zwingli, John Calvin) and to the gathered community (Anabaptists) was affirmed and was theologically substantiated. Up to the present day there is no agreement among the various Christian traditions on the relationship of worship, preaching and the sacraments.

Yet no church holds that truth is relative. Indeed, all churches recognise the authority of the Holy Scriptures; and at least for the Reformation churches, it is the task of the theologian within the community of faith to ask whether the church's praxis, including the church's worship practice, is in harmony with the ground it confesses to be true. This brings us to the question of the authority on which theological reflections and decisions are based.

The question of authority

Methodological deliberations are often tiresome. But in this case they are not only important, but necessary. They are necessary because the worship practices of the various Christian traditions—Roman Catholic, Orthodox, Anglican, Uniting, Lutheran, Baptist etc—are so ingrained in theological visions, liturgical formulas and prayer books, and, even more important, they are so deeply rooted in the hearts and minds of their adherents that one could easily come to the conclusion that worship practices are self-authenticating.

Theological reflections would then be superfluous, or they could only serve to justify, interpret and validate, but not to evaluate, the various worship practices.

An added argument for the priority of worship over theological reflection is that the worship practices of the early churches preceded the formation of doctrine and canon. Indeed, in the formation of the Christian canon, which lasted until the end of the fourth century, acceptance of the different parts of Scripture in the worship life of the churches was a necessary precondition for being accepted into the canon.

Therefore, both the history of worship and the fact that worship is so closely linked to our personal and denominational identity make it understandable and even attractive, not to evaluate and criticise it, but to consider it as given, as self-authenticating, as theologically proven and valid.

Yet that is theologically unacceptable. The worshipping community is not comprised of people who have constituted themselves to practise their religious interests. The church is called into being by the word of God! Faith and its social dimension, the Christian community, 'came' with the 'coming' of Christ into the life of believers (Gal 3:23–6). This 'coming' happened through the word, preaching Christ in the power of the Spirit (Rom 10:17; Gal 3:2, 5). Then, called into being by the word, the gathered community met for worship. It is the word of God that authenticates Christian worship and remains its measure. Not the church, not experience, however important and valuable they may be, but the word of God that speaks God's salvation into the human conscience is the centre and focus of Christian worship.

It is therefore fundamental to recognise the encounter of word and faith as the point where salvation becomes manifest.[2] Although faith comes to individuals, it does not individualise people. It restores people's relational nature by creating a community of faith. Both the individual and the community respond to the word / faith encounter with thanksgiving and worship.

The struggle for truth

By naming the wellspring, the focus and the centre of Christian worship, the question of truth is raised. Not all religious worship is true worship. Worship can fail to fulfil its *telos*. Worship itself therefore calls for its continuing evaluation. A few illustrations from the Judeo-Christian tradition underscore this point.

Although a theology of the word and a theology of atonement with the corresponding sacrificial cult practices exist alongside each other in the various traditions of the Hebrew Scriptures, a clear distinction is made between true and false worship. Preference is given to the trajectory: Word—Listening—Obeying—Implementation. 'Obeying the voice of the LORD . . . is better than sacrifice . . . ' (1 Sam 15:22). True worship of God is not to offer sacrifices, but to listen and obey God's word, to respond 'joyfully and with gladness of heart' (Deut 28:47), and to implement that commitment in the struggle for justice.

> See, I have set before you today life and prosperity, death and adversity. *If you obey the commandments of the LORD your God that I*

---

2. It is this emphasis on the proclamation of the Christ-centred word with the aim to elicit and sustain faith that the early Christian offices of apostle, prophet and teacher have in common. Compare Jürgen Roloff, *Die Kirche im Neuen Testament*. Grundrisse zum Neuen Testament. NTD Ergänzungsreihe 10, (Göttingen: Vandenhoeck & Ruprecht, 1993), 139–42.

> *am commanding you today, by loving the LORD your God, walking in his ways, and observing his commandments, decrees, and ordinances, then you shall live and become numerous, and the LORD your God will bless you in the land that you are entering to possess* . . . call heaven and earth to witness against you today that I have set before you life and death, blessings and curses. Choose life so that you and your descendants may live, loving the LORD your God, obeying him, and holding fast to him; for that means life to you and length of days, so that you may live in the land that the LORD swore to give to your ancestors, to Abraham, to Isaac, and to Jacob (Deut 30:11–20).[3]

In the New Testament the best description of an early Christian worship service is found in 1 Cor 11 – 14, and there it illustrates the apostle Paul's struggle for the identity and relevance of the gospel. What would cause the apostle to make this astonishing assertion: 'When you come together, it is not really to eat the Lord's supper' (1 Cor 11:20)? What had happened? Individualism ('. . . when the time comes to eat, each of you goes ahead with your own supper, and one goes hungry and another becomes drunk' [1 Cor 11:21]), a lack of social concern for nannies, slaves and wharf labourers who came late to the meeting (' . . . when you come together to eat, wait for one another' [1 Cor 11:33]), and a theology of sacramental security (1 Cor 10:1–5) had distorted what was later called

---

3. Other relevant passages in various traditions in the Hebrew Scriptures underscore the distinction between true and false worship and indicate the emphasis on word, obedience and justice: see 1 Sam 15:22; Is 1:11–17; Jer 7:21–8; Hos 6:6 (and compare 8:13); Amos 5:21–4; Mic 6:6–8 and Psalm 50:7–15

the Agape-meal, in the context of which the 'Lord's supper' would be celebrated.[4] Paul therefore had to remind the members of the church in Corinth that by their attitude and action they were displaying 'contempt for the church of God' and humiliating 'those who have nothing' (1 Cor 11:22). He pleads with them to recognise that the crucified Christ is the host at the Lord's supper—'the Lord Jesus *on the night when he was betrayed* took a loaf of bread . . .'—and that this fact has implications, not only for the celebration of the Lord's supper, but for the life of faith in general. It is the word, therefore, that interprets the situation and the word has its ultimate content in the crucified Christ.

As a further illustration of the struggle for true worship, we remind ourselves of the foundational Reformation critique of the Roman Catholic understanding of worship and preaching.[5] Roman Catholic worship, then and now, centres in the eucharist, and the eucharist is understood as human work and as a real propitiatory sacrifice that is offered ever again to God.

The *Catechism of the Catholic Church* (*Apostolic Constitution 'Fidei Depositum'* of Pope John Paul II [1992]), referring to the Council of Trent, formulates:

> The sacrifice of Christ and the sacrifice of the Eucharist are one single sacrifice: 'The victim is one and the same: the same now offers through the ministry of priests, who

---

4. For details, see Thorwald Lorenzen, 'The Crucified Christ as Lord of the Church: Theological Reflections on 1 Cor 11 – 14', in David Neville, editor, *Prophecy and Passion: Essays in Honour of Athol Gill* ATF Series 5 (Adelaide: ATF Press, 2002), 83–125.
5. See for instance Karl Barth, *Church Dogmatics I/1. The Doctrine of the Word of God* (1936), § 3, 71–9.

> then offered himself on the cross; only the manner of offering is different.' 'In this divine sacrifice which is celebrated in the Mass, the same Christ who offered himself once in a bloody manner on the altar of the cross is contained and is offered in an unbloody manner.'[6]

To safeguard the understanding of the eucharist as a sacrifice, the Council of Trent specifically damned other under-standings:

> If any one saith, that in the Mass a true and proper sacrifice is not offered to God . . . let him be anathema (Canon 1).[7]

> If any one saith, that the sacrifice of the Mass is only a sacrifice of praise and of thanksgiving; or, that it is a bare commemoration of the sacrifice consummated on the cross, but not a propitiatory sacrifice; or, that it profits him only who receives; and that it ought not to be offered for the living

---

6. *Catechism of the Catholic Church* §1367. The reference to the Council of Trent is to the 22nd Session, the 'Doctrine on the sacrifice of the Mass', chapters 1 and 2. The centrality of the eucharist is further elaborated in the *Catechism.* Although Christ 'is present in many ways to his Church: in his word, in his Church's prayer, 'where two or three are gathered in my name', in the poor, the sick, and the imprisoned, in the sacraments of which he is the author, in the sacrifice of the Mass, and in the person of the minister. But he is present . . . most especially in the Eucharistic species' (§ 1373). 'The mode of Christ's presence under the Eucharistic species is unique. It raises the Eucharist above all the sacraments . . .' (§ 1374).
7. Council of Trent, 22nd Session, 'Doctrine on the sacrifice of the Mass', Chapter IX.

> and the dead for sins, pains, satisfactions, and other necessities; let him be anathema.[8]

Although one detects a discernible shift of emphasis in the *Vatican II Constitution on the Sacred Liturgy* (1963),[9] the gulf between the Roman Catholic understanding with the eucharist as a human work and a real sacrifice at its centre, and the protestant/evangelical understanding that the proclamation of the gospel constitutes the church and invites Christian worship, and that in worship we receive before we act in praise and thanksgiving, is still wide and deep.[10]

The facts, therefore, that Christian worship is not its own cause, that Christian worship is controversial, and that it can go wrong, make it necessary to seek for its truth and authority outside its practice. The implications for our task are threefold:

- can we, and how can we, name the ground of faith and worship to become its ongoing measure?

---

8. *Ibid.*
9. The *Vatican II Constitution on the Sacred Liturgy* (1963) states that 'the two parts which . . . make up the Mass, namely, the liturgy of the word and the Eucharistic liturgy, are so closely connected with each other that they form but one single act of worship' (§ 56). Yet such statements occur alongside the traditional language that focuses on the centrality of the eucharist as 'the divine sacrifice' (§ 2).
10. It should be recognised, however, that since Vatican II with its new appreciation of the 'word', biblical hermeneutics has grown and blossomed within the Roman Catholic tradition. But ecclesiastical interest and practice have not kept up with the new interest on the 'word'.

- since the New Testament Scriptures contain, and in some sense are, the earliest deposits of Christian worship, we must start there.

- yet we must be aware that historical proximity does not necessarily imply theological adequacy. The earliest is not necessarily the best and truest. While it is historically interesting, and while it must also be taken seriously in theological reflection, our intent is not merely to repeat what the early Christians did.[11] Instead, we must try to correlate historical findings with our understanding of what is revealed in the trinitarian history of God.

A word of caution is in order at this point. Given the deep-seated (psychology) and fossilised (liturgical forms[12] and prayers) worship practices of the different

11. When, for instance, in 1 Tim 2:1–15 we read that in the Christian worship service 'prayers, intercessions, and thanksgivings be made for everyone', then that is clearly in harmony with the great Christian affirmation that God is the creator of all, and that in Christ, God has reconciled the world with himself (2 Cor 5:17–21), but when in the same text it is insisted that women must 'learn in silence with full submission' ('she is to keep silent'), that women are not allowed 'to teach or to have authority over a man', and that 'she will be saved through childbearing', then we must postulate a theological departure from the revolutionary assertion that salvation in and through Christ entails the abrogation of gender, class and economic divisions (Gal 3:28).
12. As an illustration we may mention the Vatican II *Constitution on the Sacred Liturgy. Sacrosanctum Concilium* (1963) where it is said that no priest 'may add, remove, or change anything in the liturgy on his own authority' (§ 22:3). Indeed the 'study of sacred liturgy is to be ranked among the compulsory and major courses in seminaries', and professors of the other disciplines must 'clearly bring out the connection between their subjects and the liturgy . . .' (§ 16).

churches, theological insights will probably make little difference and change nothing. On the other hand, if the need for theological reflection is accepted and the self-authentication of worship is rejected, then theological reflection can clear the way for the renewal of worship, even if only in the long run.

The foundation, wellspring and norm of Christian worship

With God raising Jesus from the dead and making Christ known by means of preaching—telling the story of Jesus as the story of God's universal and unconditional love and salvation—in the power of the Spirit, the new reality of the resurrection flows over into the life of believers and begins to shape their individual and community life. Through preaching, faith and baptism, believers and their communities enter the story of Jesus, not as a 'continuing incarnation'—which would relativise the uniqueness of and our need for Christ—but as causing a change of ultimate loyalty. The Christian conscience is liberated from having to shape its own identity (what the apostle Paul calls 'salvation by works') to experiencing its identity as a gift of God, celebrated in thanksgiving to God and service to the world. Christian believers are 'in Christ',[13] they 'have been raised with Christ', their 'life is hidden with Christ in God' (Col 3:1–3).[14]

God's act in Christ (the event of salvation) and the Spirit (the eliciting of faith) calls for response. The

---

13. The expression 'in Christ' is often found in Paul. It portrays the whole Christian life—living, dying, working, thinking, talking, marrying, hoping, trusting, granting hospitality—as happening 'in Christ'.

14. The new life in Christ is powerfully portrayed in the New Testament, see 1 Cor 6:11; 2 Cor 1:19f; Gal 2:19f and Rom 6:23 and 8:38f.

response of thanksgiving to God for what God has done for us is the worship-life of faith.

When the first Christians wanted to celebrate and share their newly found faith in Christ, they had the following means readily available: their *life* as individuals and as community, the *meal* with a long history of social and religious significance, and the *word* through which the God of Abraham, Isaac and Jacob has spoken to his people. Up to the present day these dimensions form the centre of Christian worship.

It remains controversial, however, which of these deserve theological priority. Life or meal and word? The meal (eucharist) or the word (preaching)? With regard to the latter it is interesting that Vatican II asserted that 'the liturgy of the word and the Eucharistic liturgy are so closely connected with each other that they form but one single act of worship',[15] but theological reflection and ecclesiastical practice tell a different story. It is clear that in the Roman Catholic Church and in certain sections of the Anglican and Uniting churches the 'meal' is more prominent than the 'word', while in evangelical Protestant and Reformed churches it is the other way round.

Keeping in mind that historical proximity does not necessarily mean theological adequacy, it is, nevertheless, informative and helpful to reflect on the situation when Christian faith began to become historically manifest.

Dimensions of Christian worship in the earliest Christian communities

It is well known that traditional Greek liturgical language like λατρεία (cultic worship/adoration) and λειτουργία (cultic service) are only used metaphorically in the New Testament (for exanmple Rom 12:1; Phil 2:17).[16] That does

15. See above, footnote 10.
16. The one exception is Acts 13:2. Otherwise, in the New Testament, religious cult language is used only for Jewish and

not mean, however, that in the earliest Christian communities there was no community worship and no community liturgy. We need to discern carefully how worship was shaped in the context of Christian faith.

In temple and synagogue

The evangelist Luke, in his story of the emerging church, says that the Jewish-Christians in Jerusalem met 'every day *in the temple* and at home' (Acts 5:42, also 2:46). Christians also participated in services at various synagogues (Acts 9:20; 13:14–42; 14:1; 17:1–4, 17; 18:5–7, 16; 19:8). Although Luke paints an idealistic picture of the early Christian church, and he also shows a theological interest in Jerusalem and its temple, there is no reason to deny that the earliest Jewish-Christians continued to worship in temple and synagogue. For them Jesus was the promised Jewish Messiah, and they witnessed to that conviction in both temple and synagogue. Jesus himself never rejected temple and synagogue worship as such, although he was critical of its deformations (Mk 11:11–19; Mt 5:23).

Yet, the tension between their newly found faith 'in Christ' and traditional Jewish worship probably soon led to a retreat from temple and synagogue to their houses. The following reasons may have motivated that change:

- temple worship entailed several sacrificial practices, while Christians began to believe that Jesus was the sacrifice 'once for all'.[17] They confessed that 'Christ had offered for all time a

---

Gentile religious services. For the Christian use of cultic language see footnote 28.

17. This theme is theologically developed in the Epistle to the Hebrews. Other texts from different traditions making the same assertion are: Rom 3:25; 6:10; 1 Pt 3:18; Mk 10:45; Mk 14:24.

single sacrifice for sins'. Their sins were therefore forgiven, and 'where there is forgiveness of these, there is no longer any offering for sin' (Heb 10:11–31)[18]

- Jesus had left for his disciples the regular practice of a common meal. This common meal became the major focus of the emerging Christian worship services in various house churches

- the Gospels of Matthew and John reveal increasing animosity, conflict and opposition between Christians and the synagogues, with Christians being identified as such and then excluded from the synagogue

We may therefore turn our attention to the other forms of early Christian worship.

In house-churches

Just as Greek-speaking Jews met in house-synagogues, so Christians met in house-churches.[19] They were exhorted 'to meet together . . . encouraging one another' (Heb 10:25). These meetings took place in the houses of richer Christians and were often led by women.[20] The worship

18. Indeed, if this is an important reason why Christians ultimately departed from temple worship, then any intimation of a repeated sacrifice in Christian worship must be vigorously resisted.
19. 'The church (*ekklesia*) in their/her/your house' is a standard expression in the Pauline corpus (Rom 16:5; 1 Cor 16:19; Col 4:15; Phlm 2).
20. Specific mention is made of Phoebe (Rom 16:1), Nympha (Col 4:15), Lydia (Acts 16:14f.40), Mary, the mother of John Mark (Acts 12:12), and Priscilla, who is often mentioned before Aquila (Rom 16:3.5a; Acts 18:18.26; 2 Tim 4:19).

service was generally conducted in the context of a meal.[21] Most probably it included the following elements:

- the 'coming together', 'assembling', 'gathering' (1 Cor 11:17–20; 14:23, Mt 18:20) for *koinonia* ('fellowship', 'intentional community', Acts 2:42).[22] Although these meetings may have taken place every day (Acts 2:46), the 'Lord's day' or the 'first day of the week' assumed special significance for these gatherings (Rev 1:10; Acts 20:7; 1 Cor 16:2)

- A meal provided the context for early Christian worship ('the breaking of bread', Acts 2:42; 20:7). Those who could afford it would bring food and wine (1 Cor 11:20f, 33f.), dedicate it to God, then share it with the gathered community. In the context of the meal, the 'Lord's supper' (Cor 11:20) was celebrated

---

21. I have analysed and interpreted the main text in the New Testament where such a meal is described (1 Cor 11–14) in: 'The Crucified Christ as Lord of the Church,' (full details in footnote 5).
22. *Koinonia* is a theologically laden concept. It has many shades of meaning. It was used by the early Christians to describe the *koinonia* within the trinity, between the believer and Christ, and of believers among each other. It also described the solidarity collection that Paul took up in Asia Minor for the church in Jerusalem. It has become an important concept for ecumenical conversations in our time. See further Thorwald Lorenzen, 'The Church as *koinonia*', in *St Mark's Review* No 172, Summer 1998: 7–13, and Thomas F Best and Gunther Gassmann, editors, *On the Way to Fuller Koinonia. Official Report of the Fifth World Conference on Faith and Order* Faith and Order Paper number 166, (Geneva: World Council of Churches, 1994).

- Prayers (Acts 1:13; 2:42; 12:12; 1 Tim 2:1), like crying 'abba father' (Gal 4:6; Rom 8:15) were spoken

- 'Hymns' and 'psalms' were sung (1 Cor 14:26; Eph 5:19; compare Col 3:16; James 5:13; Rev 5:9; 14:3)[23]

- Prophets would utter *propheteia* (1 Cor 14:6; Rom 12:6; 1 Thess 5:20; 1 Tim 1:18, 4:14; Acts 11:27; Rev 19:10), interpreting the situation in light of their understanding of the word of God (1 Cor 14:26–32; 1 Thess 5:19–21): '. . . those who prophesy speak to other people for their up-building and encouragement and consolation' (1 Cor 14:3). The gathered community would be asked to evaluate whether the spoken message echoed the confession that 'Jesus is Lord' (1 Cor 12:1–3) and witnessed to the fact that God is love (1 Cor 13 in the context of 1 Cor 11–14).

Propheteia can refer to preaching in general (Rom 10:17; Acts 10:33; 16:32; 18:7; 20:7–12) and to the more specifically evangelistic preaching of Jesus as the Christ (Acts 5:42). In Acts 10:34–48 Peter's preaching is associated with the receiving of the *Holy Spirit* and *baptism*. In Acts 11 Peter reports to the apostles in Jerusalem how in the providence of the Spirit he had the privilege of giving 'a message by which you and your entire household *will be saved*' (Acts 11:14). Paul and Silas reply to the Philippian jailor's request: 'Believe on the Lord Jesus, and you will be saved, you and your household.' They are invited to his house and there they 'spoke the word of the Lord to him and to all who were in his house' (Acts 16:31f.). 'On the *first day of the week,* when

23. Texts of such early Christian hymns can be reconstructed from texts such as John 1:1–18; Phil 2:6–11; Col 1:15–20; 1 Tim 3:16.

we met to *break bread,* Paul was holding a discussion with them; since he intended to leave the next day, he continued speaking until midnight' (Acts 20:7). Paul explains to the elders in Ephesus: 'I did not shrink from doing anything helpful, proclaiming the message to you and teaching you publicly and from house to house, as I testified to both Jews and Greeks about repentance toward God and faith toward our Lord Jesus' (Acts 20:20f.).

In 1 Cor 11:26 the meal and the word are closely interrelated: 'as often as you eat this bread and drink the cup, you proclaim the Lord's death until he comes.' 'Proclaim' here can be an indicative or an imperative, and it can mean that the 'Lord's supper' as such is the proclamation of 'the Lord's death' or that the Lord's supper includes an accompanying proclamation.[24] We need to come back to this question.

Preaching included various dimensions for the creation, shaping and sustaining of faith, and for the upbuilding of the church: 'the teaching of the apostles' (Acts 2:42); 'teaching' (1 Cor 14:6, 26; 1 Tim 4:13; Acts 5:42, 20:20); 'revelation' (1 Cor 14:26); 'tongue' (1 Cor 14:26;

---

24. CK Barrett, following Jürgen Schniewind, interprets: '. . . it seems certain . . . that it (*katangellete*) must mean *proclaim*, announce by word of mouth', *The First Epistle to the Corinthians* (London: Black, 1968), 270. So also Hans Conzelmann, *1 Corinthians. A Commentary on the First Epistle to the Corinthians*, translated by James W Leitch, Hermeneia (Philadelphia: Fortress Press, 1976), 20. The alternative is well stated by Robertson and Plummer: 'The Eucharist is an *acted* sermon, an *acted* proclamation of the death which it commemorates' (Archibald Robertson and Alfred Plummer, *A Critical and Exegetical Commentary on the First Epistle of St Paul to the Corinthians*. ICC (Edinburgh: T&T Clark, 1978), 249; also I Broer, '*katangello*' in *Exegetical Dictionary of the New Testament* (Grand Rapids: Eerdmans, 1991), 256.

further: Mk 16:17; Acts 2:4); 'interpretation' (1 Cor 14:26); 'exhorting' (1 Tim 4:13); 'admonish one another in all wisdom' (Col 3:16).

- Then there was 'the public reading of the Scriptures (1 Tim 4:13 '). Apostolic letters would also be read in a worship service: 2 Cor 7:8; Col 4:16; 1 Thess 5:27; 2 Thess 3:14

- There was the laying on of hands for blessing or ordination (1 Tim 4:14, 5:22; 2 Tim 1:6f).

- Acclamations and benedictions like 'Christ is Lord' (Phil 2:11); 'amen' (often in the Pauline epistles and in Revelation); 'our Lord, come!' (1 Cor 16:22); 'hosanna in the highest' (Mk 11:9f.); 'hallelujah' (Rev 19:1).

The diversity of early Christian worship services[25] is interesting. Not all the elements would have been present every time. But it is most likely that besides the meal character and the 'eucharist' or the 'Lord's supper' as part of it, there was preaching and different forms of verbal utterances like prayer and singing. We summarise by noting a number of dimensions that shaped an early Christian worship service.

It was *public* and as such it included the hope that 'outsiders' and 'unbelievers' may understand, 'bow down before God and worship him, declaring, 'God is really among you' (1 Cor 14:25; compare vv 16f, 23f). Transparency in communication was important. Glossolalia would therefore have to be interpreted. Withdrawal and anonymity are not concomitant with Christian faith.

25. It must be emphasised again that there was no word for 'worship service'. The simple and secular word of 'gathering' or 'coming together' was used.

The worship service was *eschatological* in that it anticipated the joy when God will be all in all and when love will have triumphed. The worshipping community would call into its presence the words of Jesus: 'Truly I tell you, I will never again drink of the fruit of the vine until that day when I drink it new in the kingdom of God' (Mk 14:25), and acclamations like 'our Lord, come!' would underscore the eschatological dimension.

The worship service echoed a *trinitarian* understanding of God in that both the saving work of Christ (his death for us) and the present reality of the Holy Spirit (preaching, faith, prayers, singing, glossolalia, laying on of hands, healings) shaped the underlying grammar of Christian worship.

By withdrawing from temple and synagogue to the house, the Christian worship service entailed a *critical and prophetic* dimension. Christians are to give their 'bodies as a living sacrifice' and they are to 'continually offer a sacrifice of praise to God' (Rom 12:1f; Heb 13:15). The 'once for all' sacrifice of Christ was not repeated but remembered and celebrated as the focus and foundation of Christian worship.

In contrast to temple (only males officiating) and synagogue (at least ten males need to be present), Christian worship could be celebrated by *two or three* (Mt 18:20; Acts 16:25) and it could be led by *women*. Furthermore, any distinction between leaders and participants was functional.

The legacy of Jesus, the elements of criticism against law, temple, sacrifice and synagogue, and the eschatological anticipation of the 'kingly reign of God' suggest that the basic atmosphere in early Christian worship services was one of joy, freedom, openness (*parresia*) and thanksgiving.

In life

A third dimension of Christian worship, clearly explicated in the early church, is the worship of God with our 'bodies', not only in temple, synagogue and church, but in our everyday life.[26] Our life in family and profession, in politics and in the sports club, all areas of our life, are potential times and places for worship.

Romans 12:1f is decisive. Paul introduces the final major section in his letter to the Roman church with these words:

> I appeal to you therefore, brothers and sisters, *by the mercies of God*, to present your *bodies* (τὰ σώματά as a *living sacrifice* (θυσιαν ζωσαν), holy and acceptable to God, which is your *spiritual worship* (λογικὴν λατρειαν). Do not be conformed to this world, but be transformed by the renewing of your minds, so that you may discern what is the will of God—what is good and acceptable and perfect.

The 'spiritual worship' mentioned here is not a cultic act like the offering of sacrifices. It is not some holy rite in which a member of a priestly class acts on behalf of and for the people. It does not take place in a specially designated sacred space. Rather, it is the grateful response ('by the mercies of God') of believers, who, by making their whole life (their 'bodies') available to God as a 'living sacrifice',[27] enable God, through them, through

---

26. Important and influential has been the essay by Ernst Käsemann, 'Worship in Everyday Life: a note on Romans 12' (1960), in *New Testament Questions of Today* (London: SCM, 1969), 188–195.

27. It is noticeable that when the early church used cultic and religious terminology, it immediately interpreted it in light of its new understanding that Jesus Christ has made the sacrifice 'once

their obedience, to make God's claim on God's creation, manifest.[28]

Conclusion

The above description has shown that close to the well-spring of the Christian faith and the Christian church, the Christian worship of God, after a relatively brief period of worship in temple and synagogue, took shape in two primary dimensions: the worship of God in *gathered communities of faith* and the worship of God in *all aspects of everyday life*.

How are these two dimensions related? Is one more important than the other? Should we say, for instance, that what we do in our Sunday worship functions to inspire and motivate us for real worship in our home and work place during the week? Or should we follow the ecclesiastical tendency to see the real worship on Sunday, which we then protect by focussing on the clergy, making

---

for all', that he has relativised the separation between holy and profane, and that therefore the whole Christian life as thanksgiving to God and as service in God's world is the appropriate act of worship. In the following texts such transformation of religious terminology can be observed: 2 Cor 9:11f; Rom 15:15f; Phil 2:17 and 4:18; 1 Pt 2:5, 9 and Hebr 13:12–16.

28. Details in Ernst Käsemann, *Commentary on Romans* (Grand Rapids: Eerdmans, 1980), 325–331, for example, 'Christian worship does not consist of what is practiced at sacred sites, at sacred times, and with sacred acts . . . It is the offering of bodily existence in the otherwise profane sphere. As something constantly demanded this takes place in daily life, whereby every Christian is simultaneously sacrifice and priest. Here the universal priesthood of all believers is proclaimed . . .' (329). Compare also Rudolf Bultmann, *Theology of the New Testament*. volume 1 (London: SCM, 1952), chapter III, §§ 11 and 13

attendance compulsory, and by excluding 'others' (whether they be other Christians or non-believers)?

The shaping of faith in early Christian communities suggests that we affirm both dimensions of Christian worship equally: worship in the gathered community of faith and worship in one's public and private life. Both are important and both are grounded in the Christ event.

This brings us to the question what role and what function preaching has in Christian worship,

The place of preaching in Christian worship

There is mainly one way to elicit Christian faith and then to keep Christian faith Christian—to introduce an unbeliever to Jesus Christ and then continually interlink faith with its ground and content, the story of Jesus Christ.

This brings us back to 1 Corinthians 11 and the argument of some theologians that the inter-relation between the Lord's supper and proclamation—'. . . as often as you eat this bread and drink the cup, *you proclaim* the Lord's death until he comes' (v 26)—means that the 'Eucharist is an *acted* sermon, an *acted* proclamation of the death which it commemorates'.[29] If that were the case, if it were evident in itself what the eucharist means, if the eucharist were self-explanatory and self-authenticating, then one can understand why some churches and their theologians exalt the eucharist over the word and claim that Christ is primarily and uniquely present in the eucharist.

This interpretation is exegetically possible, but on theological grounds it needs to be rejected.

The apostle had reminded the church in Corinth that there is no sacramental security (1 Cor 10:1–5). He had just criticised the Corinthian practice of the 'Lord's supper'. Indeed, he had just questioned whether they still

29. See above, footnote 25.

were a Christian church (1 Cor 11:20). Since he could not entertain the impossible possibility that a church can cease to be what it is, he had just suggested a compromise—'If you are hungry, eat at home, so that when you come together, it will not be for your condemnation' (1 Cor 11:34)—which, by the way, the church then institutionalised and kept to the present day.

It was therefore the *word*, telling the story of the Crucified Christ as Lord of the Church and as host at the 'Lord's supper'—'. . . the *Lord Jesus on the night when he was betrayed* took a loaf of bread . . .' (1 Cor 11:23)—that for Paul was the decisive, indeed, only way by which the Spirit corrects distortions in the worship life of Christians and in their worship services. Here in a concrete situation the apostle applies his theological conviction that

> the message about the cross is foolishness to those who are perishing, but to us who are being saved it is the power of God . . . For since, in the wisdom of God, the world did not know God through wisdom, God decided, through the foolishness of our proclamation, to save those who believe. For Jews demand signs and Greeks desire wisdom, but we proclaim Christ crucified, a stumbling block to Jews and foolishness to Gentiles, but to those who are the called, both Jews and Greeks, Christ the power of God and the wisdom of God (1 Cor 1:18–25).

We must therefore conclude that with the togetherness of meal and word, of eucharist and preaching, the theological priority must be given to preaching. Given that the crucified and risen Christ is the host at the 'Lord's Supper', the meal is the constant and tangible reminder as to whom the Christian community belongs and from where it is to receive its nourishment and vision. At the same time it is the word that interprets the situation and names what the 'Lord's Supper' is, and reveals, as Paul does in 1 Corinthians 11 – 14, when it has missed its *telos*. Only by naming the Christian community as the community of the Crucified Christ does the 'Lord's Supper' proclaim the ground and content of the Christian faith. Word and meal belong together, with the theological priority for the word.

Preaching addresses us as 'hearers of the word' (Karl Rahner,[30] Eberhard Jüngel[31]) and reminds us to whom we belong and who alone can sustain our life before and with God. We are language beings. We are spoken to before we can speak. God's word calls us into being (Gen 1; Heb 11:3), and God's 'Yes' addresses us in our situation of estrangement and calls us into 'new' being (2 Cor 1:18–22, 5:17–21). It is therefore primarily through the word that God comes to us. This is enhanced and celebrated by the *koinonia* of believers and the sacraments. But the sacraments are not self explanatory. It is the word that names them for what they are. Christ centred preaching is

---

30. Karl Rahner, *Hearers of the Word* (London: Sheed and Ward, 1969) (1941).
31. Eberhard Jüngel says: ' . . . in essence humanity is the creature *addressed* by God . . .' (*The Freedom of a Christian: Luther's Significance for Contemporary Theology* (Minneapolis: Augsburg, 1988), 65 (and see 60–65). Again: 'The being of humanity is constituted and organized by the word. We are ourselves as hearers. Only because we can hear are we able to speak, think, act, be human. As hearers we centre ourselves on God's relation to us, in order to correspond to our God'. ('Humanity in correspondence to God. Remarks on the image of God as a basic concept in theological anthropology' [1975] in *Theological Essays* (Edinburgh: T&T Clark, 1989), 145 (and see 145–8).

the theological centre of Christian worship. The following reasons intend to support that thesis.

1. *Preaching proclaims and communicates the acts of God in past, present and future*. Christian faith entails the call[32] to make known and implement what God has done for God's creation:

> you are a chosen race, a royal priesthood, a holy nation, God's own people, in order that you may *proclaim the mighty acts of him who called you out of darkness into his marvelous light* (1 Pet 2:9).

In the preaching event horizons become merged. Preaching is not less, but it is more than proclamation. The power of the gospel, which is grounded in the life, death and resurrection of Jesus, seeks through the means of preaching to become transformative in human life and human history.[33] The event of reconciliation and the witness to that event are merged into a single effective

---

32. The apostle Paul confesses: 'If I proclaim the gospel, this gives me no ground for boasting, for an *obligation* (η αναγκη = divine necessity) is laid on me, and woe to me if I do not proclaim the gospel!' (1 Cor 9:16). See also Karl Barth, *Church Dogmatics I/1* (1936), 99–101.
33. Note this helpful quotation concerning the nature of the gospel from Ernst Käsemann: '. . . gospel and preaching should not simply be equated . . . The gospel is more than the message actualized in the church. It is God's declaration of salvation to the world, which is outside human control, which is independent even of the church and its ministers, and which constantly becomes a reality itself in proclamation in the power of the Spirit. It can thus be called δύναμις θεοῦ' (*Commentary on Romans* [1980], 22).

reality. This is helpfully and clearly illustrated in 2 Cor 5:17–21:

> if anyone is in Christ, there is a new creation: everything old has passed away; see, everything has become new! *All this is from God, who reconciled us to himself through Christ, and has given us the ministry of reconciliation*; that is, *in Christ God was reconciling the world to himself,* not counting their trespasses against them, and *entrusting the message of reconciliation to us.* So we are ambassadors for Christ, since *God is making his appeal through us*; we entreat you on behalf of Christ, be reconciled to God. For our sake he made him to be sin who knew no sin, so that in him we might become the righteousness of God.

The event of reconciliation—'all this is *from God,* who reconciled us to himself through Christ'—and the ministry of reconciliation—' God . . . making his appeal *through us*'—form a theological unity.

This means that preaching is both *informing* and *performing*. It gathers up all the elements of proclaiming, teaching, comforting, inspiring, revealing, and chastising. In different ways the preacher tells the story that in Christ, God has reconciled the world with himself. At the same time, the Spirit may use that occasion to create a sacred time and divine space and liberate the human conscience to celebrate life and its giver. One might be tempted to call such preaching a sacrament if there were not the danger of dissolving Christ, the one and only sacrament, into the preaching event.

The British philosopher John L Austin[34] makes a helpful distinction between performative and constative utterances. A *constative* utterance refers to an event that has already taken place. It is there apart from the utterance. The utterance says what already is. Applied to our discussion it may, for instance state that in Jesus' death God has saved us; we only need to be informed about it. Preaching would then be imparting the information that God in and through Jesus' death has saved us. Faith would mean accepting this information as true. A *performative* utterance, on the other hand, does not merely point to an event but 'performs' an event. The utterance is a constitutive part of the event of which it speaks. The event is not complete without the utterance. This is probably what Paul meant when in 2 Cor 5:18–20 he maintains that God has called forth both the event of reconciliation and the ministry of reconciliation. And because both belong together, Paul can say that God makes God's appeal through *us*. It means that God can be effectively present in the preaching event. The hearer is not simply informed about what happened in the past, but the hearer is changed by being drawn into a language event that tells the story of Jesus as the story of God's unconditional love.

2. *Preaching aims to elicit faith*. It is by the word, including the word of preaching, that God invites faith. Preaching is anchored in the word of God for its content and effectiveness.[35]

---

34. *How to Do Things with Words* (The William James lectures delivered at Harvard University in 1955) (Cambridge: Harvard University Press, 1962).
35. We should remind ourselves of Karl Barth's helpful discussion of the 'the Word of God in its threefold Form', in *Church Dogmatics I/1* (1936), §§ 4, 98–140.

> We also constantly give thanks to God for this, that when you received the word of God that you heard from us, you accepted it not as a human word but as what it really is, God's word, which is also at work in you believers. (1 Thess 2:13)

Since 'God is ἐστίν) love', therefore God's very being is in sharing, in loving, in coming. God seeks to share God's life with us without being imposing. With Christ and the word witnessing to Christ, faith 'comes' (Gal 3:23–29), and it 'comes from what is heard, and what is heard comes through the word of Christ' (Rom 10:17)! The 'word of Christ' is the 'word of the exalted Lord . . . which manifests itself in the apostolic preaching and conversely makes this a means of Christ's self-revelation'.[36] It is hard to resist re-reading the suggestive passage in which these words are found. Salvation is found in being freed from the self and being empowered to call 'on the name of the Lord'. 'But how are they to call on one in whom they have not believed? And how are they to believe in one of whom they have never heard? And how are they to hear without someone to proclaim him?' Therefore, 'beautiful are the feet of those who bring good news!' For they have been 'sent' by God to invite people to the journey of faith (Rom 10:13–21).[37]

It is therefore in the event of the word, including the word of preaching, that faith and therewith also the community of faith is born.

---

36. Ernst Käsemann, *Commentary on Romans* (1980), 295
37. There are of course many other illustrations, like the sermons in the Book of Acts that tell the story of Jesus and therewith invite faith.

3. *Preaching is a public event.* It proclaims the good news that what God has done in Christ, God has done for all creation. Part of the saving event, the life, death and resurrection of Christ, is to 'go into all the world and proclaim the good news to the whole creation' (Mk 16:15).

The sermon therefore reveals, ever again, the mystery that life is not self-grounded but grounded in God. The 'outsider' and the 'unbeliever' fulfil an important theological function in the Christian worship service: do they understand what is taking place (1 Cor 14)? The sermon is necessary to make present the story of Jesus in such a way that the mind can understand and the heart can perceive.

Since God loves the world (John 3:16) and indeed has reconciled the world with himself (2 Cor 5:17–21), therefore preaching aims to interpret the 'world' from the perspective of the word of God. This includes teaching how the content of faith relates to modern life, pastoral care reminding us of the spiritual resources that are available to help us carry our burdens and heal our wounds, and the prophetic dimension unmasking and denouncing that which is inhuman and therefore not concomitant with the Christian vision of life.

Finally, to make preaching public, the community of faith is a constitutive part of the preaching event. By listening and responding, the community provides the context for others to listen and respond.

4. *Preaching witnesses to the 'new creation'.* The preacher must seek to preach the gospel as gospel, as *good* news, reflecting the radical and unconditional 'yes' of God. The story of Jesus through which the ministry of the Spirit invites faith in the believer is primarily *a story of joy and freedom*. The 'kingly reign of God' is closely associated with joy (Mt 13:44–46; Lk 15:4–7, 9f.), and 'where the Spirit of the Lord is, there is freedom' (1 Cor 3:17; compare Gal 5 and John 8). The sermon brings our life

into correlation with the message that our real identity lies in the discovery that we are creatures, created, sustained and called by a God who is interested in us and who wants us to be 'fellow workers' (1 Cor 3:9) in God's economy. 'Where the gospel corresponds to Christ, and the messianic fellowship of the people corresponds to the gospel, the truth of the proclamation is recognized from the freedom it creates'.[38] Christian worship celebrates the divine gift of joy and freedom. 'Joy is the actualisation of freedom, which takes concrete form in fellowship . . .'[39] Consequently, the Christian worship service is the 'event of freedom' just as worship in everyday life is the 'implementation of freedom in the ministry of love'.[40] All elements of the worship service, including preaching must echo the liberation that God has given with the Christ-event.

5. Given that 'the inclination of the human heart is evil from youth', as the Jahwist perceptively said long ago (Gen 8:21), faith needs to be *sustained* and it needs to be protected against *many distortions*. The following are some fairly common distortions of faith:

- by *politicising faith,* Christians have fought crusades, burned heretics, blessed weapons of war and used the word 'God' to justify and

38. Jürgen Moltmann, *The Church in the Power of the Spirit* (1977), 226.
39. Hans Conzelmann in 'xai/rw ktl.' *Theological Dictionary of the New Testament* IX (1974: 359–76) 369. Likewise David Buttrick in *Homiletic Moves and Structures* (London: SCM, 1987), 454: 'Preaching is essentially a *good* news that liberates.'
40. Eberhard Jüngel, 'Der evangelisch verstandene Gottesdienst,' in *Wertlose Wahrheit. Zur Identität und Relevanz des christlichen Glaubens. Theologische Erörterungen III* (München: Kaiser, 1990), 283–310, 309 (my translation).

further their own national, political, economic and other ideological causes

- by *individualising faith,* believers have failed to recognize that although faith comes to individuals, it does not individualise people. Faith takes place within a community, and it calls and shapes people into a community of faith

- then there is the *emotional distortion of faith*. Faith has, of course, emotional elements, but faith must not be reduced to human experience

- even the *church* can hinder faith by claiming to become the object of worship and obedience: not the church, but Jesus Christ is the ground, object and content of faith

- faith must also not be confused with *reason*. For the Christian, reason is a servant of, not a master over, faith. Faith is not against reason, but it is much more encompassing than reason

- there is also a *moralistic distortion of faith*. Faith includes obedience. Faith entails content and structure. But both the Ten Commandments ('I am the LORD your God, who brought you out of the land of Egypt, out of the house of slavery . . .' [Ex 20:2]), and the Sermon on the Mount ('Blessed are you . . .' [Mt 5:3ff]), teach us that obedience and morality are grounded in the liberating activity of God

- and, finally, there is the *cultic distortion of faith* when the 'once for all' sufficiency of Christ's

> work of reconciliation is relativised by understanding worship as human work in which Christ is offered again as a sacrifice to God.

It is the role of preaching in the wider celebration of the worship service—and only preaching can fulfil this function!—to protect faith against the above distortions by ever again inter-relating our life and situation with the story of Jesus.

6. *Preaching has a prophetic responsibility.*[41] If with the apostle Paul we want to preach 'Christ crucified',[42] we cannot overlook the fact that Jesus was opposed, captured, tortured, sentenced and executed for certain reasons. To do so would de-historicise Jesus and deny the incarnation. Jesus did not die of a heart attack or of old age. His death was not the result of a judicial error. Jesus was opposed and ultimately killed as a result of his conflict with the economic, political and religious forces of his day.[43] To call this Jesus 'Lord' implies that one must enter the struggle between the world and God. Christian preaching must name the demons of our time and then seek to mobilise Christians to take up their cross and follow Jesus into the market-places of life. It needs to be a continuing and stern reminder to Christians at all times and in all places that the apostle Paul questions the Christian identity of the church in Corinth because in its worship services the church had forgotten that closeness

41. Roger Alling and David J Schlafer, editors, *Preaching as Prophetic Calling. Sermons that Work XII* (Harrisburg: Morehouse Publishing, 2004), has a good introduction to the challenges and pitfalls of prophetic preaching (ix–xiv).
42. 1 Corinthians 1–2. The same theological emphasis is made by the evangelist Mark in Mark 8:27 – 9:1.
43. For details, see Thorwald Lorenzen, *Resurrection, Discipleship, Justice: Affirming the Resurrection of Jesus Christ Today* (Macon: Smyth & Helwys, 2003), chapters 3 and 7.

to Jesus must always entail compassion and solidarity with the 'wretched of the earth'. Therefore, besides being evangelical, telling people that Jesus is their saviour, priestly, reminding people that Jesus is their friend, and teaching people the grand story that in Jesus God is sharing the human story, preaching includes also a prophetic analysis and judgment of the things of the world.

The preacher and her/his message

What I have said above entails the suggestion that the preacher must be prepared to become part of the preaching event. Not as the content of the sermon, but as the medium that is willing to echo the one word of God, Jesus Christ. Preachers must be willing to accept responsibility for what they proclaim. 'For we are not peddlers of God's word like so many; but in Christ we speak as persons of sincerity, as persons sent from God and standing in his presence' (2 Cor 2:17).[44]

Christian preaching can therefore not be separated from Christian *witness* (Greek *martus* from which the English 'martyr' derives).[45] The witness stakes her life on the event to which she witnesses and as such becomes part of the event. The witness keeps an event alive. At the same time the event must shape the life of the witness and thereby assigns kerygmatic dignity to the life of the witness. The apostle Paul therefore modifies his tradition by refusing to objectify the cross. He speaks of cross and resurrection in existential categories by interpreting his life with all its difficulties christologically: '. . . always

44. It may also be helpful to remember the biblical injunction: 'anyone, then, who knows the right thing to do and fails to do it, commits sin' (James 4:17).
45. Compare Lorenzen, *Resurrection, Discipleship, Justice, op cit*, 144–46.

carrying in the body the death of Jesus, so that the life of Jesus may also be made visible in our bodies' (2 Cor 4:10). The same is true for the evangelist Mark, for whom the proper response to Jesus is not merely the verbal confession that 'Jesus is the Christ', but the existential preparedness to take up one's cross and follow him (Mk 8:27–9:1).

This raises the important but controversial question whether and in what sense the life of the preacher —her/his preparedness to accept personal responsibility for what they say—is part of the preaching event. One is reminded of the famous saying of Martin Luther: 'What does not teach Christ is not apostolic, even though St Peter or Paul taught it; again, what preaches Christ would be apostolic, even though Judas, Annas, Pilate and Herod did it'.[46] And contemporary theologians agree: '. . . the sanctification of the theologian is not constitutive for the situation of proclamation.'[47]

One cannot help being sympathetic with the intention of this insistence. If the validity of the gospel were to depend on the sanctification of the preacher, who then could preach? Are we not all sinners who 'fall short of the glory of God' (Rom 3:23)?

It is also important to safeguard the hermeneutical principle that the Scriptures are their own interpreter (*sacra scriptura sui ipsius interpres*), so that the biblical message is not determined by our individual or ecclesiastical interests. The exegete is a servant of the text and must resist the ever-present temptation to become master over it. But being a servant of the text includes the

46. *Preface to the Epistles of Saint James and Saint Jude* 1545 (1522), in *Works of Martin Luther* The Philadelphia Edition (Philadelphia: Muhlenberg Press, 1932) volume VI, 478.

47. Eberhard Jüngel, *Predigten* Kaiser, München 1968, 129 (my translation); also David Buttrick, *Homiletic Moves and Structures* (London: SCM, 1987), 456–59.

willingness to be drawn into its reality. Ernst Fuchs asserts correctly that 'even the most pious talk of God without our involvement is atheistic',[48] and WD Just says: 'While in scientific statements one must generally aim for the highest measure in content and objectivity, in religious language games 'objective' talk (sachliches Reden) without personal participation is an "offence against the rules".'[49]

Recalling the paradigm in Mark 8, Peter's orthodox confession 'You are the Christ,' is rejected by Jesus. Even the demons can make such propositional statements (Mk 3:11, 5:7). Only he who denies himself, takes up the cross and follows Jesus can know Jesus as Son of God, and can therefore responsibly confess: 'You are the Christ'.

This is no presumptuous claim or moral demand for the sanctification of the preacher, nor does it make the validity of God's salvation dependent on human performance. But it does suggest that the content and the effectiveness of the gospel are at stake in the preacher's existence. If, to use an example, preachers tell the story of Jesus as the story of God's love, but show no desire to incarnate it in their own existence, then the message in its content and effectiveness is compromised. God has limited himself to make the obedience and performance of God's 'fellow workers' a necessary part of accomplishing God's plans. Preachers therefore bring their own existence

---

48. *Jesus. Wort und Tat* JCB (Tubingen: Mohr, 1971), 94 (my translation) and compare 105; likewise James Wm McClendon, Jr, *Systematic Theology, volume II: Doctrine* (Nashville: Abingdon, 1994), 399f.
49. *Religiöse Sprache und Analytische Philosophie* (Sinn und Unsinn religiöser Aussagen) Kohlhammer Stuttgart 1975, 152 (my translation).

into the preaching event; whether God uses the message is not at the preacher's disposal.

Conclusion

God in the power of the Spirit and through the preaching of the gospel invites faith and calls the community of faith into being. Christian life and its social dimension, the church, are therefore grounded in the word of God.

When the word of God arrives, it liberates the human conscience and restores the *humanum* from its individualistic and self-centred distortion to be relational and to find its identity in relationship to God, to fellow human beings and to nature.

In response to God's word, the believer and the community of faith give thanks to God and celebrate life—they worship. This worship takes place in two spheres, the everyday sphere of life and in the Christian community sphere where Christians regularly and publicly meet for worship.

This was originally done in the context of a meal. Today the meal has been replaced by the gathered community and by the Lord's supper, eucharist, holy communion. Yet to keep faith centred in Christ, to safeguard worship as a response of joy and freedom, rather than human work, and to assign proper meaning to the sacraments it is the preaching of the gospel that keeps Christian worship Christian. This is why preaching is central to Christian worship.

5
Worship and Preaching: An Orthodox Christian Perspective

Romanos Stergiou

Introduction

The Orthodox Church remains one of the few Christian churches today that practices its worship with great symbolism, tradition, and ritual. For it is within the context of worship that the church's Holy Tradition, history, and even the Holy Scriptures, are borne. Preaching is an integral part of Orthodox worship, because it is the way in which the Word of God is proclaimed to God's people.

Through the following pages, allow me to share with you some thoughts on how the Orthodox Church views the place of preaching in worship, and how worship produces the place, content, and atmosphere for preaching.

Worship in the liturgical tradition of Orthodox Christianity

The aim of Orthodox worship is and has always been not only to commemorate but to express the holy actions of human salvation contemporaneously in a sanctified atmosphere. The 'sanctified atmosphere' referred to here is found in the Divine Liturgy, the Holy sacraments and other liturgical offices. Through the Liturgy the believer experiences the manifestation of God's glory, the *kenosis* of the Son, and reflects the Trinitarian act of love through love for his neighbour.

In addition, worship, dogmas and even theology have always been actualised within the context of this 'sanctified atmosphere'. According to Archimandrite Vasileios, 'Outside the framework of the Divine Liturgy . . . it is impossible to understand Orthodox faith and theology'.[1]

For Orthodox Christians, worship constitutes the combination of heaven and earth during the Liturgy. The opening words, 'Blessed is the Kingdom of the Father, and the Son and the Holy Spirit, now and ever and to the ages of Ages', express this belief and move the believer towards a spiritual transcendence from earth to heaven. It is through the liturgy that we are prepared to receive the Word of God.

The reception of this Word in worship is a sacramental experience and accomplished 'theanthropically'. Since it is the belief that heaven and earth come together in worship, the mystical dimension of worship is combined with a cognitive and sensual dimension. Ioannis Fountoulis[2] refers to this as *logiki latreia* (a reasoning-meaningful worship) where the worshipper experiences and comes to an understanding of the *Logos* mystically by God's grace and by using all cognitive senses.

> According to Paul the Christian must 'pray with the spirit . . . pray with the understanding . . . sing with the spirit, and ... sing with the understanding' (1 Cor 14:15). If this rational dimension of worship is missing, if the one who sings does not know the

---

1. Archimandrite Vasileios (Gondikakis), *Hymn of Entry*, translated by Elizabeth Briere (Crestwood, New York: SVS Press, 1984), 30.
2. Ioannis Fountoulis is Professor of Liturgical Theology at the University of Thessalonica and is considered a leading scholar in his field among the Greek Orthodox academic fraternity.

> 'meaning of the language' (14:11) if the believer does not understand that which is being spoken, then he will be—according to Paul—'speaking into the air' (14:9). Worship then becomes an irrational worship or a type of magic.[3]

Thus, when entering an Orthodox Church, worshippers are immersed in this *logiki latreia.* They see the Word expressed on the walls, hear the Word in the readings and chanting, smell the Word in incense, touch the Word by venerating it, and taste the Word by receiving His very body and blood.

Liturgical preaching in Orthodox worship

As mentioned above, Orthodox Christianity worships God and receives His Word sacramentally. With the reception of God's Word there must also be a proclamation of God's Word. Among the various forms of proclamation, none is more relevant to the contemporary worshipper than preaching, which participates in and is an extension of the Liturgy. Since preaching is a mystical and sacramental act, its purpose is to lead the people into the sacramental experience of the Word in worship.

Preaching in worship is also God's way of directly speaking to His people through His chosen 'vessels', to which we will refer later. According to Fr Thomas Hopko: 'The Homily at a Divine Liturgy . . . is a unique Word of God that has never been spoken or heard before and will never be spoken and heard again'.[4] Preachers must therefore be aware that even though the words expressed

---

3. Ioannis Fountoulis, *Logiki Latreia* [in Greek] (Thessalonica: Apostoliki Diakonia, 1984) (second edition).
4. Fr Thomas Hopko, 'On Preaching in Church', in *Speaking the Truth in Love* (Crestwood, New York: SVS Press, 2004), 49.

in a sermon are theirs, God's personal message is being delivered at that particular point and according to the needs of that congregation. Since preaching is God's personal message to His people, it must be a discipline which strives to be devoid of human weakness and intellectual pursuits. Fr Hopko describes clearly what a sermon should not be:

> The liturgical sermon, therefore, is not missionary evangelising, catechetical teaching, biblical exegesis, theological instruction, spiritual direction, or pastoral counselling, though it must be connected to these inspired tasks . . . It is most certainly not the preacher's time for baring his soul, sharing his troubles, revealing his burdens, grinding his axes, or taking vengeance on his enemies.[5]

Even though a sermon is not any of the above, preaching disciplines must refer to tasks such as biblical exegesis and must consciously follow the legacy of the church Fathers. We will discuss the patristic legacy further on, but let us now discuss Orthodox biblical exegesis and its use in worship and preaching.

Exegesis and liturgy

As biblical exegesis is one of the major inspired tasks of preaching, it too is based in the Liturgy. In Orthodox Christianity, the Bible is interpreted not so much in a purely cognitive sense but as part of the celebration of the Divine Liturgy. Congregants experience Scripture and its interpretation primarily as a liturgical celebration and secondarily in their private reading and study. Private reading is encouraged and practised, but its interpretation

5. *Ibid*, 50.

comes via liturgical worship. Fr John Breck explains this further by saying:

> The Word of God is sacramentally communicated in corporate worship, and this has primacy over individual acts of reading. Through confession and absolution followed by Eucharistic communion, the participant experiences the Word actualised via the nourishing worship of the ecclesial community.[6]

In addition to liturgical celebration—the element of biblical exegesis in the present—Orthodoxy is very conscious of simultaneously referring to the past by faithfully studying the Apostles and the Fathers of the church. Since there was no finalised canon of the Bible in the apostolic era, a Holy Tradition of interpretation was established and passed on by word of mouth within the church. Without this wisdom of the Church of the past, biblical interpretation in the present loses its true historical message. George Cronk explains that the full meaning of Scripture can be illustrated '. . . only from within the historical unfolding and expression of faith of the church, and only from the standpoint of holy tradition in its entirety'.[7] Thus, the Protestant model of biblical exegesis, *sola scriptura,* has never found its way into Orthodox hermeneutics or preaching.

Orthodox hermeneutics also emphasises that biblical interpretation is properly fulfilled only with the guidance of the Holy Spirit. In another article, Fr Hopko states that:

---

6. John Breck, *The Power of the Word in the Worshiping Church* (Crestwood, New York: SVS Press, 1986).
7. George Cronk, *The Message of the Bible: An Orthodox Christian Perspective* (Crestwood, New York: SVS Press, 1990), 24.

'Exegesis in the Holy Spirit, in the context of fulfilment, is the only method of exegesis which the church has for its Bible'.[8] If the Word witnesses the saving acts of God, and the church lives them sacramentally, it is the Holy Spirit that makes it all possible and becomes the hermeneutical influence of the church. The Holy Spirit—who bears Divine authority and truth—is therefore the source of all authority and truth in Scripture and the church.

> However, when He, the Spirit of truth, has come, He will guide you into all truth; for He will not speak on His own authority, but whatever He hears He will speak . . . (John 16:13).

According to Fr George Florovsky, the church, guided by the Holy Spirit is 'the only authentic depository of Apostolic kerygma'.[9] Only within the church do we seek an authentic interpretation of the Scriptures, since the church forms the sacred depository of truth, and since the Word is proclaimed and preserved there. Preaching must therefore be inspired by the Holy Spirit, draw from Holy Tradition and the Fathers, and be exercised within the liturgical worship of the church.

Preaching and the Fathers of the church

After the apostolic era, other dynamic preachers rose in a 'show of power of the Spirit' (1 Cor 2:5) to proclaim the Word of God to the next generation. These preachers, referred to as the 'Fathers' of the church, would,

---

8. Thomas Hopko, 'The Bible in the Orthodox Church', in *St Vladimir's Theological Quarterly*, volume 14, numbers 1/2 (1970): 82.
9. George Florovsky, *The Collected Works, Volume 1: Bible, Church, Tradition* (Vaduz Europa: Büchervertriebsanstalt, 1987), 89–90.

throughout the centuries, preach about the truth of our faith and how it leads to salvation. Their aim in preaching was to convince people to become living members of the body of Christ, and images of the 'invisible God' (Col 1:15).

Orthodox theology believes that consistency in the didactic message of different Fathers in different ages, from the Apostles until today, is the work of the Holy Spirit diachronically. This consistency is referred to as *consensus patrum,* and this consensus of the Fathers constitutes the church's conscience. Archbishop Stylianos has eloquently expanded on this theological concept by referring to it as the church's *phronema*:

> Therefore, in teaching the truths of the faith, the individual person is able to have the same assistance from above to believe correctly, if he or she in good conscience struggles to remain in undisturbed communion and spiritual accord with the body of the church, and especially with the *phronema* of the church Fathers (*consensus patrum*).[10]

For many non-Orthodox Christians, frequent reference to the Fathers is not a priority. So why do Orthodox use the Fathers so extensively in preaching and biblical exegesis? Metropolitan Emilianos Timiadis answers this question succinctly:

> The fathers as a whole reflect the teaching of the undivided church in general. They were not seen just as eminent theologians or highly

10. Archbishop Stylianos Harkianakis, 'Dogma and Authority of the Church', in *Phronema* (Annual Review of St Andrew's Greek Orthodox Theological College, Sydney), volume 12 (1977): 13.

> qualified doctors of theology; they were also esteemed because of their depth, their unique spirituality, their life in prayer, their theological consistency, holiness and accuracy.[11]

The Fathers of the church are therefore considered as the heralds of the Holy Spirit and perpetual teachers of the gospel, not because of their teachings alone, but also because they are seen as supreme embodiments of the life of Christ. A conscientious preacher, in following Paul's appeal to 'imitate' (1 Cor 4:16) him, will continue to imitate and immerse themselves into the church's *phronema* as part of their preparation to preach, while remaining faithful to the *consensus patrum*. But a conscientious preacher will also immerse themselves in the life of the church, and live their faith in Christ as well.

One of the greatest of all the Fathers, well known for his eloquence in preaching, was St John Chrysostom, Patriarch of Constantinople. Of all his works, none is more popular than *On the Priesthood*. In the fourth book, he says that preaching is not a discipline but an embodiment of the Word: 'We must take great care, therefore, that the Word of Christ may dwell in us richly'.[12] We must therefore understand clearly that in order for biblical exegesis and preaching to be executed faithfully the preacher must live the faith. John Breck states that proper or 'orthodox' interpretation of scripture 'requires on the part of the interpreter a life of personal repentance, ascetic struggle and worship'.[13] In addition to

---

11. Metropolitan Emilianos Timiadis, *The Relevance of the Fathers* (Brookline: Holy Cross Orthodox Press, 1994), 4.
12. St John Chrysostom, *On the Priesthood* IV, 3.
13. John Breck, *Scripture in Tradition: The Bible and its Interpretation in the Orthodox Church* (Crestwood, New York: SVS Press, 2001), 31.

proclaiming the Word and glorifying God, Orthodox patristic tradition requires the preacher to go beyond living the faith and to have a 'vision' of God. St Irenaeus of Lyons states: 'The glory of God is the living man, and the life of man is the vision of God'.[14]

Towards a 'theoria' (vision) of and encounter with God in preaching

When one reads the Bible, one is confronted with what seem like paradoxes. The concept of a *theoria* (vision) of God is one such example. In the book of Exodus we are told that 'You cannot see my face, for man cannot see me and live' (33:20). Conversely, though still in the Pentateuch, the book of Genesis contains the following antithesis: 'I have seen God, face to face, and yet my life is preserved' (32:30). This antithesis of the visibility and invisibility of God has throughout the centuries been explicated by Fathers such as St Gregory of Nyssa, St Symeon the New Theologian, and Maximus the Confessor. None however explain the topic with more clarity than the fourteenth century Father, St Gregory Palamas.

Following the tradition of the Fathers before him, Palamas explains that in order to understand the antithesis between the visibility and invisibility of God, a distinction must be made between God's *ousia* (essence) and God's *energiai* (energies). As Vladimir Lossky explains, 'St Gregory Palamas resolves this antinomy, without suppressing it, by preserving the deep-rooted mystery which dwells intact within the ineffable distinction between the essence and its natural energies'.[15] Man is incapable of participating in the

14. St Irenaeus *Against the Heresies* 4,20,7.
15. Vladimir Lossky, *The Vision of God* (Crestwood, New York: SVS Press, 1983), 156.

essence of God due to his fallen human nature, but out of God's love, man participates in the energies which God communicates to him. By understanding this distinction, preachers can therefore comprehend certain mystical experiences of God's revelation without denying the incomprehensibility of God.

Under the Palamite synthesis, a 'vision' of God is possible, and so man is able to encounter God in variable degrees. Bishop Kallistos Ware informs us that 'to worship or to pray is to stand before God . . . this implies that worship is an encounter, a meeting between persons' and that the purpose of worship is 'to enter into a direct and personal relationship with God the Holy Trinity'.[16]

When preparing a liturgical sermon, it is necessary for preachers to have a 'vision' of God and to encounter Him through their personal prayer and corporate worship. When preparing their sermon, preachers must 'pray without ceasing' (1 Thess 5:17) and encounter God, not only for their congregation but for themselves as well.

The relationship between worship and dogma expressed in preaching[17]

Dogma in the Orthodox Church has a deep interrelationship with worship, because it is the experience of the church which has produced it. Before there were any dogmatic formulae, or even a New Testament, the Divine Liturgy already existed and was practised by the early church. Since dogma is a source and the result of the church's liturgical life, it is only within the context of worship that it finds its grounding.

16. Bishop Kallistos Ware, *The Inner Kingdom* (Crestwood, New York: SVS Press, 2000), 59.
17. See Archbishop Stylianos Harkianakis, *Dogma and Ethos as Source and Resultant of Divine Worship*, in Greek at present. A translation of this article is currently in progress.

> Dogma is the expression of the mystical life of the church . . . [and] Dogmas do not concern just the experts; they give guidance and are a prerequisite for life; they lead unerringly to the fullness of life in the Holy Spirit.[18]

As explained above, preaching is connected to the inspired tasks used to fulfil its purpose. Since theological instruction is one of these tasks, preaching must also remain faithful to the dogmatic truths which have been incarnated from the church's worship life. Bishop Hilarion states that 'Orthodox worship is the incarnation of dogmatic truth through the words of prayer'.[19] It is in the liturgy that one will find basic Christian teachings being experienced through prayer.[20] It is also in the context of worship that preaching has its incarnation and must express the proclamation of God's Word dogmatically.

Transfiguration and preaching

Before we begin to speak about the preacher, we must make a distinction between preaching and the aforementioned Liturgical preaching. All who are baptised sacramentally, in the name of the Holy Trinity, are members of the 'royal priesthood' (1 Pet 2:9). As part of their responsibilities, each baptised member of the church is therefore, a 'preacher' and must 'preach the gospel of

---

18. Archimandrite Vasileios, *op cit*, (at footnote 1 above), 19.
19. Bishop Hilarion Alfeyev, *The Mystery of Faith* (London: DLT, 2002), 168.
20. As an example, the Nicene Creed, which contains the dogmatic truths of the undivided church of the first millennium, is still prayed in the Divine Liturgy and other divine offices of the Orthodox Church.

peace' and bring 'glad tidings and good things' (Rom 10:15).

The power of the gospel of Jesus Christ dwells within preachers. This power not only dwells but flows from preachers, transfiguring them and everything around them. Some feel that it is not necessary for them to speak out verbally about the gospel and thus lessen the witness of the royal priesthood. However, all believers are subject to the Lord's parables and should 'not hide their lamp under a bushel, nor lose the flavour of their salt'. Those baptised in the Lord should submit themselves to the transfiguration they have undergone and should bear witness to it, in word and in action.

In addition to the responsibility of preaching by the royal priesthood, there is a preaching ministry bestowed on the ordained priesthood through the laying-on-of-hands[21] referred to earlier as Liturgical preaching. This enables the bishop—or other clergy appointed by him—to speak out 'rightly teaching the word of truth' not only in a secular setting, but also in the sacred atmosphere of the Divine Liturgy from the pulpit. For it is the ordained ministry who have been called to bear this unique seal of the gift of the Holy Spirit expressed in Liturgical preaching.

The ordained preacher, however, must know what to preach. He must know it first in his own heart and live it in his own life. Even though the gift of preaching is bestowed at ordination, this does not guarantee the quality of preaching. For some a 'special grace' (1 Pet 4:10) is obvious and this talent is used to proclaim the Word without much effort. For others, however, they must work more diligently in making sure that the message is untainted by their own weakness. Even though the power of the Word of God is eternal and incorrupt, the quality of

---

21. See John 15:16, Acts 6:6, Titus 1:5.

preaching is directly related to the effort expended by the preacher.

The place and time of preaching in Orthodox tradition

We mentioned above that the physical place of Liturgical preaching is from the pulpit, during worship. As for the time in which it should be delivered, Professor Foundolis explains that 'the only appropriate time for the delivery of the sermon is immediately after the Gospel reading'.[22] The preacher may find the need, however, to change this to just before the Benediction if there are any sincere pastoral concerns.

The readings prescribed for the services are based on an annual cycle and must be maintained. The practice of maintaining this established 'calendar' of biblical readings has made such an impression on Orthodox Christians that they can identify seasons and Sundays with names of parables and thus give added meaning to their daily lives. For example, you may hear them referring to the Sundays preceding Great Lent as the 'Sunday of the Publican and the Pharisee' or the 'Sunday of the Prodigal Son'. Consequently, the content of the liturgical sermon will be based on the readings of that day.

Final thoughts on worship and preaching

As we have argued until now, an active sacramental life is imperative to both the preacher of the Royal Priesthood and the Ordained Priesthood. For the early church, Christian worship preceded the formulation of scripture and dogma. The New Testament was written, to a great degree, within the context of the Liturgical life of the early church. In this sense, the dynamic interrelationship

---

22. Ioannis Fountoulis, *Homiletike* (in Greek) (Thessalonica: Melissa Publications, 1994), 128.

established by the life of the early church between Scripture and Liturgy must continue, so that preaching remains faithful as the authentic proclamation of God's Word.

For nearly 2000 years the liturgical life of the church has been the context in which the worship, doctrine, history, and spirituality of Christian experience have existed. It is through the Liturgy that preaching feeds the flock, calls to repentance those who lose their way, and assists in converting new sheep through Holy Baptism. Adopting a minimalist approach to the Liturgy reduces the wealth of experience and tradition which is so integral to the mission of preaching.

The liturgical tradition of the church constantly provides renewed ways of proclaiming the Word in preaching. It is in the best interests of the preacher to be a part of the worshipping body of Christ because worship 'provides the pivot around which the spiritual life of a believer revolves'.[23] Most importantly, the Liturgical sermon not only proclaims the Word of God to those being preached to, but also to the preacher.

---

23. Ioannis Fountoulis, *Leitourgika Themata* volume 3 (in Greek) (Thessalonica: Melissa Publications, 1977), 51.

6
Going to Church and Being the Church

Anthony Gooley

Gathering for worship on Sunday has an ecclesial and Eucharistic context that is sometimes not fully understood, even in communities which have maintained the Eucharist as the focus of Sunday worship. There is a certain tendency in much of 'Western' culture toward a kind of individualism which is shared by many Christians that obscures the ecclesiological dimension of the Sunday gathering. The experience of worship can be enhanced by the development of a deeper understanding of the reality signified by the gathered community. An ecclesiological understanding is necessary in order to shift the mindset of worshipers from one of going to church to one of being the church. Such a shift has implications not only for the experience of worship but also for leading the congergation deeper into the mission of Christ in our world. The Church understood as communion opens the way to engaging in worship as a dynamic and present encounter with the mystery of the presence of God and the possibility of transformation of communities and our world.

In order to commence our discussion it is necessary to consider the framework of the paper. Three phrases need to be considered, what we mean by 'going to church', by 'being the church' and by 'communion ecclesiology'. Going to church can be characterised as an emphasis on reception of a service or a personal faith experience. As long as Christians gathered for worship regard 'being at church' on Sunday as an essentially private affair they will fail to experience the reality of the gathering. Going to church is then a continuation of the cultural paradigm of individualism. Attendance at Sunday worship will be perceived as a gathering of individuals, who as faith filled people, could offer the same effective prayer alone just as much as with a community. There is no doubt that the Spirit can move individuals to sincere and effective prayer but this is not the same objective experience as the Sunday gathering. The Lima Statement of the World Council of Churches gave encouragement to an ecclesial understanding of Sunday worship and linked that worship to the celebration of the Eucharist: 'it is in the eucharist that the community of God's people is fully manifest'.[1] Although all Christian traditions have not maintained the Eucharist as the focus of Sunday worship, the ecclesiological principles that shed light on the significance of the Sunday gathering for worship may still find application.

'Being the church' is characterised as awareness that the the church is a community instituted by Christ and called into being and constituted by the Holy Spirit.[2] A communion ecclesiology permits that paradigm shift whereby the gathered community may recognise that they are called together in fellowship in the life of the Trinity and with each other. The fellowship of love transforms Christians and impels them to serve the world with which they feel a profound communion in the hopes and anxieties and struggles of all people, in fact nothing that is genuinely human fails to find an echo in their

---

1. World Council of Churches *Baptism, Eucharist and Ministry* Faith and Order Paper no 111, Geneva 1982 (referred to as BEM hereafter) Eucharist 19.
2. John Zizioulas [Metropolitan John of Pergamon], *Being as Communion: Studies in Personhood and The Church* (New York: St Vladimir's Seminary Press, 1985), 132.

hearts.[3] Gathering for Sunday worship, for the eucharist, becomes the experience of the reality of this communion manifest in the assembly and the worship of the whole community. This understanding of gathering on Sunday is counter cultural. Without denying individual difference and giftedness, a sense of being the church, of *koinonia*/ communion, and encounter with this mystery, inaugurates a transformation of individuals into 'a people, a kingdom and priests to serve our God' (Rev 5:10).

An ecclesiology of communion develops an understanding of the church which is profoundly scriptural and attested to in the 'great tradition' of the church. Communion has vertical and horizontal dimensions. The church is a mysterious vertical communion between God and believers and a horizontal communion among believers.[4] The communion among believers is not limited to the individual scale, it includes communion of communities of believers. The church 'is a communion, a fraternity of persons. This is why a personal principle and a principle of unity are united in the church'.[5] The community of the church has an existence prior to individual membership and it exists as a given for the context of faith and worship for individuals. The image of the church described in Acts 2:42–7, albeit idealised, attests to the communion that existed within the Jerusalem community. The community is united in a communion founded on sharing in common faith founded on apostolic witness, prayer and the breaking of bread.

---

3. *Gaudium et Spes* no 1, English translation in Austin Flannery *Vatican II: Conciliar and Post Conciliar Documents* (Dublin: Dominican Publications, 1981).
4. Michael Lawler and Thomas Shanahan, *The Church: A Spirited Communion* (Collegeville: The Liturgical Press, 1995), 3.
5. Yves Congar, *I believe in the Holy Spirit*, *Volume II*, translated by David Smith (New York: Crossroad-Herder, 1983).

Concern for the material welfare of the members and the love they have for one another is a fruit and gift of the communion created by the Spirit among them.

The New Testament and the eucharist

There is a growing consensus among biblical scholars, representing a variety of Christian communities, that the context for the reception as for the reading of the New Testament writings is the Sunday eucharist.[6] Kereszty concludes that 'the entire New Testament has a eucharistic provenance and, therefore, must be interpreted in a more or less immediate Eucharistic context'.[7] The implications of this are, he notes, that we have a Biblical foundation for a theology of the eucharist which must necessarily combine elements of christology, ecclesiology and eschatology rather than keep them separate from one another. If this view is accepted then we must also see that the church is not merely a faith community with a gathering of subjective states of mind and self expression, but a eucharistic community in which acts of faith refer to sacramental realities.[8] The church is constituted as a Eucharistic and ecclesial reality from its moment of institution unto the present.

The Eucharist provides a context for the reception of the Word of God proclaimed in the Scriptures. The assembly of the faithful becomes the means by which the individual participates in the unfolding pattern of salvation. The community is nourished by word and

---

6. Two excellent sources on the developing consensus are Roch Kereszty, editor, *Rediscovering the Eucharist: Ecumenical Conversations* (New York: Paulist Press, 2003) and Horton Davies *Bread of Life and Cup of Joy: Newer Ecumenical Perspectives on the Eucharist* (Grand Rapids: Eerdmans, 1993).
7. Roch Kereszty, 'The Eucharistic Provenance of New Testament Texts', in Kereszty, *op cit*, 44
8. Kereszty, *ibid,* 45.

sacrament. The individual is immersed in the sacramental reality of the community called the church, the body of Christ. It seems that from the beginning this corporate identity shaped the life of the individual member and drew her/him closer into the mystery of Christ present among us. Imagining these first Christian communities gathering before dawn on the first day of the week to hear the writings of the New Testament should provide a way into interpreting the word in our day.

Christ and communion

An overly individualistic understanding of going to church misses the significance of the meaning of being the church. Paul tells us in many places that the church is the body of Christ (1 Cor:12:27), that Christ is the head of his body the Church (Col 1:18) and that all that we do should be done for the building up of the body of Christ (Eph 4:13) and he reminds us with directness and beauty that ' . . . the cup of thanksgiving for which we give thanks is a participation in the blood of Christ . . . and the bread that we break is a participation in the body of Christ (1 Cor 10:16). We see here the interweaving of christological, ecclesiological and Eucharistic themes. The reality for which the community is assembled and which it encounters in the Holy Spirit is a communion with Christ in the Eucharist and the eucharistic assembly. The eucharistic communion with Christ who nourishes the life of the church is at the same time communion with the body of Christ which is the church.[9] One cannot be in Christ without being a part of his body.

Evaluations of the church which consider it as an institution only and perhaps a floored one at that or as a purely human reality will miss the significance of the

---

9. BEM Eucharist 19.

pneumatological nature of the church, that it is a community made one in Christ through the Spirit. To misunderstand the church in this way would create an obstacle to full and active participation in worship because the worshiper is not conscious that she/he encounters Christ present in the community assembled (the *synaxis*) nor is she/he seeking to engage with Christ through his body which is the church. If worship is reduced even further to a purely private encounter with the divine, an individual experience, then such worship cannot really contribute to the edification of the church. The worship of the community is impoverished by an impoverished understanding of the nature of the church and the assembly. This is not to say that individuals and communities will gain nothing from, or contribute nothing to, meaningful worship. According to Barclay, Christian *koinonia*/communion is that bond which binds Christians to each other, to Christ and to God.[10] Without such a consciousness of *koinonia* there will be something lacking in the disposition of those who come to worship. They may not discern the body of Christ in the assembly.

The eucharist and communion

It is in the eucharist that the community of God's people is fully manifested.[11] The presidential prayer preserved in the *Didache* indicates how profoundly worship and community were linked in the ancient church:

> As this broken bread once dispersed over the hills, was brought together and became one loaf, so may thy church be brought

10. William Barclay, *A New Testament Word Book* (London: SCM, 1955), 72.
11. BEM Eucharist 19.

> together from the ends of the earth into thy kingdom[12]

Zizioulas suggests that there is an abundance of evidence from historical and liturgical fragments of the early centuries of Christianity to 'allow us to know, the whole church dwelling in a certain city would come together mainly on a Sunday to break the bread. This synaxis would be the only one in that place, in the sense that it would include the whole church'.[13] It may strike some as odd that we need to consider the eucharist *and* communion because for many communion is regarded as a synonym for the eucharist. It is, I would argue, necessary to engage with the many meanings of communion/ *koinonia* in order to appreciate fully the communion that the Eucharist brings about.

Roman Catholic theology as expressed in *Lumen Gentium* regards the church in Christ as in the nature of a sacrament, a sign of communion with God and of unity among people.[14] The church is gathered by Christ as a visible sacrament of the saving unity brought about by the unique redemption and gift offered in Christ.[15] The church is regarded as being a visible society and a spiritual community, having an earthly as well as a heavenly dimension. Together these human and divine elements combine to form one complex reality. For this reason the church may be compared to the mystery of the

---

12. George Every, *Basic Liturgy* (London: The Faith Press, 1961), 72.
13. John Zizioulas, *op cit*, 150.
14. *Lumen Gentium* (hereafter LG, English translation in Austin Flannery, *Vatican II: Conciliar and Post Conciliar Documents* (Dublin: Dominican Publications, 1981), no 1.
15. LG 9.

incarnate Word.[16] There is a mystical and sacramental dimension to the life of the church which is the life of God in some mysterious way. The *Faith and Order Commission* of the World Council of Churches points to this reality, without defining it a way that would identify it exclusively with the theological tradition and language of any particular community, by saying that 'belonging to the church means living in communion with God through Jesus Christ in the Holy Spirit'.[17]

Liturgy, which includes Sunday worship, is always seen as the work of 'Christ the priest and of his body the church', according to Roman Catholic teaching in *Sacrosanctum Concilium*.[18] The ministerial priesthood and the common priesthood of the body of Christ, of the church, are both participations in the one priesthood of Christ.[19] Roman Catholic theology speaks of the real or true presence of Christ in the church, especially in the liturgy. He is regarded as being present in four ways.[20] He is present in the assembly, wherever two or three are gathered in his name (Matt 18:20). He is present in the Scripture proclaimed, since it is he himself who speaks when the word is proclaimed. He is present in the person of the presider: it is the same Christ who offered himself on the cross who is now offering through the ministry of the priest. He is present in the consecrated bread and wine, which is a participation in his body and blood (1 Cor 10:16). BEM expresses this last point, saying that 'the church confesses Christ's real, living and active presence in the eucharist'.[21] Without entering into any discussion

16. LG 8.
17. BEM Ministry 1.
18. *Sacrosanctum concilium* (hereafter SC, English translation in Austin Flannery, *Vatican II: Conciliar and Post Conciliar Documents* (Dublin: Dominican Publications, 1981), no 7.
19. LG 10b.
20. SC 7.
21. BEM Eucharist 13.

of how that presence might be effected, BEM is content to reflect that Christ's mode of presence in the eucharist is unique.[22] Gathering for worship is not primarily the recreation of a historical drama of the Lord's Supper, but a participation and encounter with Christ in the sacramental presence experienced in four modes within the *synaxis*.

Gathering together as a communion has present, past and future dimensions that suggest that the worshiping community is participating in a reality greater than individual devotion or personal faith experience. Worship points most clearly to the communitarian nature of salvation and the communitarian nature of the God from whom salvation comes and to whom all creation is drawn. To gather for worship is to be brought into the experience of communion with God and the body of Christ, the church. This communion occurs in this present moment, with the communion of Christians of all times and ages, and with the heavenly community, the New Jerusalem. Sunday worship must be situated in this larger context of communion in order to recover and experience the reality for which we have assembled.

The communion that exists in the Sunday community is not a communion limited to the present experiences of community or communion with Christ in his body the church. It is an encounter with, and anticipation of, eschatological realities. The earthly community is an epiphany of the heavenly mystery of the church, particularly in the celebration of the eucharist.[23] Recalling the eucharistic provenance of the New Testament we can see the author of the Letter to the Hebrews speaking to the eucharistic assembly when he writes: ' . . . what you have come to is Mount Zion and the city of the living

---

22. BEM Eucharist 13.
23. SC 41.

God, the heavenly Jerusalem where the millions of angels have gathered for the festival with the whole church in which everyone is a first born son and citizen of heaven' (Hebrews 12: 22–3). Those who have been baptised into Christ exist then with a kind of dual citizenship, existing at the same time on earth as members of the pilgrim church and in heaven as members of the heavenly community (Col 2:20; 3:1–4; Phil 3:30). Our participation in the eucharist already gives us a foretaste of Christ's transfiguration of our bodies . . . our bodies which partake of the eucharist are no longer corruptible but possess the hope of the resurrection.[24] The *Catechism of the Catholic Church* relates the eucharist to the coming of the Kingdom:

> The Holy Spirit's transforming power in the eucharist hastens the coming of the Kingdom and the consummation of the mystery of salvation. While we wait in hope the Spirit causes us to anticipate the fullness of communion with the Trinity. Sent by the Father who hears the epiclesis of the church, the Spirit gives life to those who accept him and is, even now, the guarantee of their inheritance.[25]

The assembly is an experience of communion with the saints and the Church that is to come as well as with the living Church gathered in the present.

Solidarity and communion with the body of Christ in the world is an aspect of eucharistic communion that is sometimes overlooked in an individualist understanding of the Sunday gathering. All kinds of injustice, racism, separation and lack of freedom are radically challenged

24. *Catechism of the Catholic Church* (hereafter CCC) §1000.
25. CCC §1107.

when we share in the body and blood of Christ.[26] If the eucharist makes us into the Body of Christ then we cannot ignore him in the poor, the refugee, and the marginalised of this world. To the extent that we turn away from the least of these marginalised people we turn away from Christ and to the extent to which we encounter the marginalised we encounter the body of Christ (Matt 25:31–46). It was a truth which seemed so obvious to John Chrysostom 'that he found it odd that people would provide precious vessels to hold the body and blood of Christ while neglecting the poor, who are the body and altar of Christ in the community'.[27] To meet Christ in the assembly is to begin to participate in the transformation of the oppressive circumstances that cause poverty and injustice, the proclamation of the kingdom of God.

The essence of the Eucharist is that it is an act of communion, the creation of a community, by the power of the Spirit, which draws life from the body in order that it might become that body. There is a mutual interrelation of the eucharist and the church, an active principle, constantly forming the reality.[28] Referring to the work of Henri de Lubac, Wang notes that the purpose of sacraments is to unite those on whom they act effectively into a union with one another and with Christ.[29]

---

26. BEM Eucharist 20.
27. Patricia Zirkel, 'The Body of Christ and the Future of the Liturgy', *Anglican Theological Review* Summer 81/3 (1999): 467.
28. Lisa Wang '*Sacramentum Unitatis Ecclesiasticae*: the Eucharistic Theology of Henri de Lubac' *Anglican Theological Review* 85/1 (Winter 2003): 154.
29. Wang, *op cit*, 145.

Formation in communion

Sacrosanctum Concilium regards Roman Catholic pastors as having a duty to 'ensure that the faithful take part fully aware of what they are doing, actively engaged in the rite and enriched by it'.[30] It is a duty which pastors in other traditions might also feel is part of their responsibility. If we are to accept that the Sunday assembly is an experience of a profound communion which operates on a number of levels then some formation of congregations will be required. An appreciation of Sunday worship as communion does not come naturally in a culture which emphasises individuality and individualism in religion, as in so many other aspects of life. The Eucharist is a primary symbol of Christian faith for most Christians. Leaders of communities need to undertake some formation of congergations to 'enable people to enter into the primary symbols of Christian faith so that they may experience in liturgical worship a union between rite and faith which will illuminate their whole human existence'.[31]

An understanding of the assembly as *koinonia*/ communion in the body of Christ has significant conesquences for ecumenism. If the Sunday assembly in a particular place is a participation in the body of Christ, then it is a participation in the communion of all the assemblies scattered throughout the globe, since Christ is one. There is one Lord, one faith and one baptism and one God the Father of all (Ephesians 4:4–6). The communion among assemblies remains an imperfect one because we do not yet share the one cup and the one bread. Returning to a sense of the church, of the Sunday assembly, as communion, can be an important preparation for a foretaste of the full communion to which we are called in

---

30. SC 11.
31. Louis Weil, 'Community: the Heart of Worship', in *Anglican Theological Review* 82/1 (Winter 2000): 131.

the Spirit. De Lubac calls this a return to an understanding of the church as the great eucharistic 'miracle'. The church is the glorious fruit of the awesome transformation that happens in the sacrament, in which we are made into that which we partake, the body of Christ.[32]

Communities might need to return to central texts of Scripture and to the witness of the Christian communities of the first centuries of the Christian era to ponder the nature of the assembly and to develop an ecclesiological understanding of the Sunday gathering which is an experience of *koinonia*/communion. Weil comments on the lack of a symbolic sense in the imagination of American culture, an observation that might well apply in the Australian context also.[33] A task for pastors is to stimulate this symbolic sense, a kind of sacramental imagination, so that the individualist understanding can give way to a communitarian understanding of the nature of the Sunday assembly. So long as this imagination remains un-stimulated, congregations will be comprised of individuals who are going to the church in a privatised manner, not aware that the gathering, the *synaxis*, is the experience *par excellence* of communion in Christ, a communion which impels toward service of the world. There needs to be a consciousness of being the Church and of the church as a way of being. In becoming more conscious of their dignity as the body of Christ, the baptised who assemble on Sunday will enter more fully into both the incarnate Word and the world which God loved so much that he sent that Word to save it (John 3:16).

---

32. Wang, *Sacramentum Unitatis*, 153.
33. Weil, *op cit*, 131.

7
This is My Body, Given For You

Timothy Radcliffe OP

Jesus taught them with authority, not like the scribes and Pharisees. How may our words be invigorated with a spark of that authority and power? How can we refresh our language of faith, so that people do not keel over in boredom when we preach? I remember once receiving a letter from a friend of mine who said, 'Dear Timothy, I am writing this letter during the sermon. I am literally weeping with the boredom of it.' I am happy to say that I was not the preacher!

In my first essay in this volume,[1] I looked at the meeting of Moses with the burning bush in the wilderness as an event that might help us to see what it means for us to meet the living Word and be changed by it. This fearful and inarticulate man was sent by the voice of the Lord back into Egypt, to confront Pharaoh and lead his people into the Promised Land. This suggests that our proclamation of faith is not so much the communication of information. It is an event, the sharing of the happening of grace. We share our encounter with the Word which is always there before us, waiting for us, whose power is weakness and which promises us a homecoming. We try to help people encounter what Cornelius Ernst called 'the genetic moment', the creative, liberating explosion of grace in our midst.

Today I wish to take the next step up the spiral staircase, to use Karen Armstrong's image, and look at an even more fundamental event in our Christian story,

1. Chapter 1 above, 'Do Not Put Out The Burning Bush'.

which is the Last Supper. This is the moment when Jesus grasps that most fundamental happening, which is his death and resurrection, and makes it a gift. Here we see language at its most transformative, 'This is my body, given for you'. It is as if our human vocation to be speakers of words finds here its climax and fulfillment. All talking aspires to the power and authority of these words. The older I become, the more I come back to them as making sense of all that we do and live. So my thesis is that one way of refreshing, re-animating (literally 're-ensouling') our preaching is to go back to that happening of grace. How can our preaching recover its dynamism?

I shall glance at three moments:

1. The Last Supper is the moment when the future collapses, and there is no story to tell of what is to come. Jesus embraces this moment.
2. He gathers the disciples into communion.
3. He reaches out for the fullness of the Kingdom.

The preaching of the church needs to be touched by each of these moments if it is to regain authority. Our words need to recover their sacramentality. There is a sort of rhythm to these steps, something like breathing, which is needed to give life to what we say.

The disappearance of the future

I suppose that when the disciples went up to Jerusalem, they still had a story that they could tell of the future. Perhaps they hoped that Jesus would reveal himself as Messiah, that Israel might overthrow the Romans, that the Kingdom might come. As the disciples on the road to Emmaus confessed to Jesus: 'We had hoped that he was the one to redeem Israel' (Luke 24:21). Whatever story they told collapsed on the night of the Last Supper. Judas had sold Jesus; Peter was about to betray him. Most of the other disciples would flee in fear. Faced with his passion and death they had no story to tell. They are reduced to silence. And, in the synoptic gospels, what Jesus does is not to offer another story, in which it will all be all right. He performs a sign, the breaking and sharing of the bread.

Paradoxically, our foundational story, which gathers the church together every Lord's day, is of the moment when there is no story to tell of the future. In fact it is starker than that. We look back to the gospels for their accounts of this moment, and it is arguable that the gospel accounts themselves derive from the second crisis of hope in the church, which was Jesus' failure to return in glory. I believe that Mark's Gospel has its origins in the acute crisis of the early seventies, when Christians suffered persecution, the first followers of Jesus were murdered, and in Rome Christians betrayed each other to the authorities. All that could sustain believers then was the imminent coming of the Lord. He must be on his way. But he did not come. Another story crashed to the ground. Or rather Jesus did come, but in a new and utterly unexpected way, in the Gospels of Matthew, Mark, Luke and John.

Every Sunday the Christian community gathers to renew its memory of our origins, 'Do this in memory of me'. But our story takes us back to when there was no story. And it does so in words born in the second crisis of hope, when it became clear that Jesus's return was not imminent. So, Christian hope does not depend on any story that tells us of the future.

The crisis of our time is often seen that of the loss of utopia. I was sustained for most of my time by the optimism of the age. Things were getting better. But really since the fall of the Berlin Wall, we have been confronted with the disappearance of the future. As Oliver Bennet has argued in *Cultural Pessimism: Narratives of Decline in the Postmodern World,* the West is suffering from a collective depression. We can see growing violence in our cities, the collapse of civil order, growing inequality between the rich and poor, the spread of Aids, the threat of ecological disaster and, above all clashes between religions and the spread of terrorism.

In the European summer of 2004 I went to Auschwitz for the first time. Early in the tour one sees a map which shows how the camp stood at the centre of a network of railway lines, which could carry people from all over Europe to their death. The lines stretched from Norway down to Greece, to Vichy France, and to the eastern front. And the lines come to an end at Birkenau. They simply stop, with the gas chambers on either side. This is literally the end of the line. This is where all our brilliant technological efficiency led. What is so strange is that it took so many decades for humanity to take on board that awful termination and to register its horror. It is as if it was only forty years after the closing of Auschwitz, that it became recognised as symbolic of our lost future.

At this moment we are offered perhaps just two stories to tell of the future. One is a scientific story, which goes from the Big Bang to the Big Chill, which can only look forward to the moment when the universe will either collapse in on itself or else go cold and dead. It is a story that offers no hope, and in which humanity cannot play a significant part. And now, recently, we have learned another story to tell of the future, which is the war on terrorism, which promises endless violence. What might ever count as winning?

This loss of story does not mean that people are necessarily miserable, though there is an epidemic of suicides by young people from Ireland to Japan. We may eat, drink and be merry, because tomorrow we may die. But the merriment may only anaesthetize our empty hearts. As in the Book of Lamentations we may feel that there is no way forward: 'He has blocked my ways with hewn stones, he has made my paths crooked' (3:9).

Faced with this loss of utopia, the eucharist does not offer some easy optimism, a happy story about what is to happen next. We Christians have no more idea than anyone else what the next hundred or thousand years hold for humanity. We cannot open the book of Revelation and say, 'Hey guys, five plagues down and two to go'. It confronts us almost brutally with the collapse of dreams, so that we may learn a deeper hope given in the breaking of bread.

Surely the beginning of our preaching lies in this silence, when all the grounds for facile optimism are destroyed and the easy little stories cease to work. I confess that I often keep going by looking forward to the next little treat: the next holiday, the next meal with friends, the next film or bottle of wine. I am carried forward day to day by little promises of fun and pleasure. I have measured out my life if not with coffee spoons, then at least with small treats. Towards the end of my time as Master of the Dominican Order I discovered that there was a relationship between the number of windows in Basilica church in Rome, called Santa Sabina, and the remaining months of my term. I would measure the progress towards my liberation from office, and future years of irresponsibility. We are sustained by such little stories, and thanks be to God for them. But the eucharist takes us back to a moment when they all collapsed and invites us to be rooted in the deeper dark soil of God's promise.

A friend of mine, my publisher, lost his wife and son in a terrible car accident. He spent months in hospital, and dreaded the visits of chaplains, whose false consolations filled him with anger. He could only begin to heal when a young chaplain said to him, 'Robin, I have no idea what to say. I am lost for words.' We have nothing at all to say until we have nothing to say. It is only when we have to beg for a word, that preaching can begin.

He took bread and broke it

Faced with the silence of the disciples Jesus, in the synoptic gospels, takes bread and breaks it and shares it: 'This is my body, given for you.' It is a creative act, in which Jesus grasps this painful moment. He is indeed to be handed over by his friends into the hands of his enemies. His words and gestures say clearly what is happening and through those words and gestures he transforms this betrayal into gift. He grasps this moment in which the community implodes, and makes of it a new covenant.

So preaching begins in being reduced to silence, which is the silence of our contemporaries faced with a threatening future. The next thing the preacher must do is grasp where it is that we are. He or she must name the moment, as Jesus does at the Last Supper. He lays hold of this moment as a moment of grace. He says clearly what is happening. If our words lack authority and power then it is because so often we fear to tell the truth. As Mary Catherine Hilkert OP writes, we fear to name the grace and the disgrace at work in our world.[2] We hesitate to bring to shared word the raw experience of those with whom we live. This is implicit in the very meaning of the bread and the wine that we share.

Geoffrey Preston OP wrote:

> Think of the domination, exploitation and pollution of man and nature that goes with bread, all the bitterness of competition and class struggle, all the organised selfishness of tariffs and price-rings, all the wicked oddity of a world distribution that brings plenty to some and malnutrition to others,

---

2. *Naming Grace: Preaching and the Sacramental Imagination* (New York: Continuum, 1997).

> bringing them to that symbol of poverty we call the bread line. And wine too—fruit of the vine and work of human hands, the wine of holidays and weddings . . . This wine is also the bottle, the source of some of the most tragic forms of human degradation: drunkenness, broken homes, sensuality, debt. What Christ bodies himself into is bread and wine like this, and he manages to make sense of it, to humanise it. Nothing human is alien to him. If we bring bread and wine to the Lord's Table, we are implicating ourselves in being prepared to bring to God all that bread and wine mean. We are implicating ourselves in bringing to God, for him to make sense of, all which is broken and unlovely. We are implicating ourselves in the sorrow as well as the joy of the world.[3]

If we do not find words for what our people really live, then how can we ever find each other in the gospel? Our communities include young people struggling to reconcile their hormones and the teaching of the church on sex, and perhaps failing to do so; the married and the divorced and remarried, the straight and the gay, old people facing retirement and solitude, those for whom the church's doctrines seem incomprehensible, people filled with anger at the church and others with what they see as the betrayal of the tradition, people facing sickness and death. Are our words touched by their experiences? Do we dare to speak aloud what they live so that they may recognize

3. *God's Way to be Man* (London: Darton, Longman & Todd, 1978), 84.

their experience in our words and so know that they belong and are at home here?

Barbara Brown Taylor reports the complaint: 'I wish preachers did not lie so much'.[4] It is not so much that preachers tell blatant lies. It is rather that sometimes we fear to grapple with the complexity of human experience. If we really acknowledge the joys and the sorrows of humanity, then we will find ourselves lost for easy words. Our ecclesiastical language will appear threadbare and inadequate. Seamus Heaney writes of an old Eskimo woman who was asked why the songs of her tribe were so short. She replied, 'because we know so much'.[5]

The eucharist is the sacrament of our home. We are gathered around the altar. This implies a proclamation of the word in which we recognise ourselves and our experience, and in which we hear the truth of what we live and feel. So that, as Barbara said, if I say 'I' others may be able to say, 'me too'. This is more than a matter of personal anecdote, a charismatic testimony to my experience of conversion. Our articulation of our faith has to create a common home in which others may feel that they belong. Our preaching must create an hospitable space in which we can meet each other, which is more than the preacher's personal experience.

One of the earliest great preaching missions of the Dominican Order, in collaboration with the Franciscans, was 'The Great Devotion' of 1233.[6] Most of the cities of northern Italy were suffering from clashes between factions and were virtually in civil war. 'The Great Devotion' was a preaching of peace. Often the climax of

4. *When God is Silent* (Boston: Cowley Publications, 1998), 107.
5. Seamus Heaney, *The Redress of Poetry* (London: Faber and Faber, 1995), 175.
6. See Augustine Thompson OP, *Revival Preachers and Politics in Thirteenth-Century Italy: The Great Devotion of 1233* (Oxford: Oxford University Press, 1992).

the sermon was a ritual kiss of peace exchanged between enemies. As preachers the friars were often authorised to ordain the release of prisoners, the forgiveness of debts, and even to rewrite the civil statutes. The test of the authority of the preached word was that it brought peace, demolished divisions, reconciled enemies. The most radical example is that of St Francis making peace between the citizens of Gubbio and the wolf. He mediates, accepting the verbal pledge of the citizens and the non-verbal language of the wolf: 'the wolf knelt down and bowed its head, and by twisting its body and wagging its tail and ears it clearly showed to everyone that it would keep the pact it had promised'.[7]

Most of us are not called to such radical mediation! One of the most beautiful experiences that I ever had of the link between peace and preaching was during a meeting of the Dominican Family in Tucuman, in the north of Argentina. I had not realised that it was Malvinas Day, when the whole of Argentina commits itself to win back the Malvinas Islands—what the British call the Falklands—from the invaders. The city was filled with Argentinean flags. At first I felt rather alone. But when I arrived at the hall to meet a thousand of my brothers and sisters, there was a little Union Jack on the desk awaiting me. I concelebrated the eucharist with the Provincial, and we prayed for all the dead, Argentinean and British. By providence I had chosen to preach that day on non-violence. It was a moment of grace and the happening of a common home.

God sends Moses back to Egypt. 'Come, I will send you to Pharaoh, that you may bring forth the children of

---

7. *St Francis of Assisi, Writings and Early Biographies: English Omnibus of the Sources for the Life of St Francis*, edited by Marion A Habig, (Chicago: Franciscan Herald Press, 1972), 1350–1.

Israel out of Egypt' (Exod 3:10). Preaching summons people out of whatever small prisons they may inhabit, into the wide-open spaces of God. Words of grace are the happening of the Father's home in which there are many mansions.

I have the impression that the church in Australia, as in the United States and much of Europe, is suffering from a degree of polarisation. You know better than I do how liberals and traditionalists are split, each having their own periodicals, their own gurus, their own bishops and seminaries. These are battles that in some places, and shockingly, have even reached the altar rails and the eucharist, the symbol of unity. The temptation of the preacher may be to make the sermon yet another launching pad in the battle. Each side has its pulpits from which to despatch its missiles against the foe. In the seventeenth century, when Jesuits and Dominican were locked in terrible battles about grace, the pulpit was called, 'the lectureship in revenge'.[8] We must not shrink the church to the smallness of our hearts and minds. This is in contradiction with the very nature of preaching, which is to create the wide-open spaces of God in which we may all belong. How might we work for this?

Moses makes the journey back into Egypt, into the servility and the bondage of those whom he has left. Jesus reaches out in covenant to those who will betray him and deny him. How do we reach out across the divisions which crucify our church, and try to touch and be touched by the imagination of those who see differently than ourselves? Let me be quite specific. There are forms of hard and intolerant rightwing Catholicism that I find deeply unattractive. They seem to me to be sectarian. For me they are an alien land. Do I just rail against them? Or dare I try to enter that land of the imagination, and

8. JS Cummins, *A Question of Rites: Friar Domingo Navarrete and the Jesuits in China* (Aldershor: Scholar Press, 1993), 46.

discover what is cherished there, what is loved and why? And what is feared? The philosopher Iris Murdoch said that when you meet someone whom you do not understand, ask of what are they afraid. This asks of us what Aquinas called a *latitudo cordis*, an expansion of the heart.

In *Larry's Party* the Canadian novelist Carol Shields explores how language offers us a home to live in. Larry's first marriage broke up because he and his young wife did not have a language that was large enough for them to find and love each other. Finally when they are reconciled it is because their language is spacious enough for them to be together for the first time. Larry asks, 'Was that our problem? That we didn't know enough words?'[9] One challenge for preaching in the West today is learning enough words, other people's words, so that God's wide open home can be spoken. Every proclamation of the faith should extend the vocabulary a little, open another window, stretch the heart a bit wider. This is the event of the Word, the happening of grace, knocking down the walls of hatred. It is a work of the imagination, of sympathy.

Towards the end of *A Midsummer Night's Dream*, Theseus says,

> . . . as imagination bodies forth
> The forms of things unknown, the poet's pen
> Turns them to shapes, and gives to airy nothing
> A local habitation and a name (Act 5 scene 1).

That is the preacher's task, to extend the heart and mind, to create a shared habitation.

---

9. Carol Shields, *Larry's Party* (London: Fourth Estate, 1998), 336.

There is a problem. This most 'Catholic' task, of seeking words with which to build a common home, will often be seen by ideologues on either side as a betrayal, as weak compromise. When Cardinal Bernadin made his brave initiative to look for the 'Common Ground', ideologues on the right rejected it, because the truth must not be compromised. Error has no rights, as we used to say. But ideologues on the left may also be indignant. When I wrote in the United States about the need to move beyond polarisation, I was roundly attacked by a well-known theologian for not laying the blame where it belonged, on the Vatican. If we preachers try to let our words be touched by the vastness of God, then we shall be attacked and misunderstood. This is part of the vulnerability of the preacher.

And so with the cup

Mark's gospel then reads, 'And he took a cup, and when he had given thanks he gave it to them, and they all drank of it. And he said to them, "This is my blood of the covenant, which is poured out for many. Truly, I say to you, I shall not drink again of the fruit of the vine until that day when I drink it new in the Kingdom of God"' (14:25).

In both Matthew and Mark we hear of the bread which is given to them and the cup which is poured out 'for many'. In all three synoptic gospels, the cup points forward to the kingdom, when all of humanity will be gathered in. So the Last Supper has a dual focus. It is the gathering of this little group of disciples around the Lord, sharing the bread. But the cup reaches out to that larger community, which is the kingdom. It is, as we say in the eucharist, 'for you and for all'. We have a similar tension in John's account of that last evening. He gathers around him those whom he calls his friends, to whom he has made known everything. But in chapter 17 he says, 'I do not pray for these only, but also for those who believe in me through their word, that they may all be one: even as thou, Father art in me and in thee' (17:20).

And so this points to an intrinsic tension within the eucharistic community. We gather around the altar as the disciples of Jesus. We are his community. But we are only truly the Lord's community if we are always stretching beyond ourselves to the fullness of the kingdom, in which all will belong. It is almost as if fidelity to the cup always subverts every community that we ever construct. It is only sacramental of the Kingdom if it is being undermined, opening its doors, reinventing itself. This tension is inherent in the very idea of Roman Catholicism. We are a particular community, whose unity is in communion with the See of Rome. We are not a vague movement of people who vaguely love Jesus. But our Catholicism reaches out to a fullness of communion, which subverts every exclusion.

The whole history of the church is fuelled by this tension. Its most dramatic moment was the admission of the Gentiles. Another such moment was the discovery of the New World, and the admission of people who had never before heard of Christ. One thinks of the words of the Spanish Dominican, Antonio de Montesinos on that First Sunday of Advent in 1511, when he rebuked the Spaniards of Hispaniola for their treatment of the indigenous people. 'Are they not human? Do they not have rational souls? With what right do you make war upon them? Are you not obliged to love them as yourselves?'. The Spanish community that was gathered around the altar had to die to its established Western identity, be opened up beyond itself otherwise it would cease to be a sacrament of the vastness of the Kingdom and just become a sign of European culture.

So the accounts of the Last Supper are held taut in a tension between the gathering into communion and its subversion. And this is a tension which surely inhabits our words. I suggested above (in speaking of the bread) that our words must create a home in which we may dwell with our fellow Christians. We do this by speaking the truth, by daring to speak of things as they are. We have to name the grace and the disgrace that are among us, the victories and defeats that we do actually live through. And we must stretch our hearts and minds to those with whom we disagree, find new words for a larger home. So here the stress is on telling the truth.

But the cup which is poured out for many, the cup of the Kingdom, offers us another challenge! We are reaching out for the fullness which is beyond imagination. The mystery defeats our words. Herbert McCabe OP wrote: 'Our language does not encompass but simply strains towards the mystery that we encounter in Christ . . . The theologian uses a word by stretching it to breaking point, and it is precisely as it breaks that the communication, if any, is achieved.'[10]

Stretching language to breaking point is a poetic task. It is poetry that renews our language by pushing it beyond what can be said easily and literally. This is beautifully described by Seamus Heaney who writes of 'its function as an agent of possible transformation, of evolution towards that more radiant and generous life which the imagination desires'.[11] He describes a poem by Dylan Thomas as giving 'the sensation of language on the move towards a destination in knowledge'.[12] We can preach the Kingdom in language that is on the move towards a destination in knowledge, as we stretch our minds and words towards a fullness that cannot be captured. Heaney even describes this poetic function in a way that is highly evocative of the eucharist itself:

---

10. *God Matters* (London: Geoffrey Chapman, 1987), 177.
11. *Op cit,* [footnote 5 above] 113f.
12. *Ibid*, 141.

> We go to poetry, we go to literature in general, to be forwarded within ourselves. The best it can do is to give us an experience that is like foreknowledge of certain things which we already seem to be *remembering*. What is at work in this most original and illuminating poetry is the mind's capacity to conceive a new plane of regard for itself, a new scope for its own activity.[13]

This foreknowledge which is also a remembering suggests the dynamic of the eucharist which is both a remembrance—'Do this in memory of me'—and also a promise of an unsayable future.

So our preaching of the kingdom requires the renewal of our language by poets and artists. Not every preacher is a poet but we need language that is kept alive, electric, tense and vibrant by poets. And this is a profound reason for the crisis of preaching today. The poetic imagination is marginal within our dominant scientific culture which tends towards a deadening literalism, a 'dry yeastless factuality'.[14] In most traditional societies, poetry, myth, song and music have been central to the culture. In our society these have often been reduced to mere entertainment. The hunger for the transcendent is still there in the human heart. As St Augustine said, it is restless until it rests in God. But in our society it is harder for the preacher to evoke that ultimate human destiny which transcends our words. If the preaching of the word of God is to flourish, then we need poets and artists, singers and musicians who keep alive that intuition of our ultimate destiny.

---

13. *Ibid*, 159.
14. Yann Martel, *The Life of Pi* (Edinburgh: Canongate, 2002), 64.

Conclusion

Preaching is in a crisis today. It needs to recover the dynamism of the Last Supper. It must be renewed as a happening of grace. And I have suggested three moments in that happening. There are surely others but I must stop soon!

First of all, the Last Supper is a moment in which the story is lost. There is no story to tell of the future. We too live through such a moment, in which we have lost our dreams and hardly dare to think what is coming next. The Last Supper may give us the courage to face that hopelessness, and to live its silence. We do not need to fill our hearts with little stories of imminent satisfaction. The Last Supper offers its sure hope now. Our preaching must dare face and embrace that dark silence, as Jesus did before his death, and await the promise.

The bread that Jesus shares with the disciples gathers them into community. This is what our preaching must do, by honestly speaking of what we live, of our human victories and defeats. We must dare to speak truthfully, in a church which is often timid and afraid and prefers to take refuge in ecclesiastical platitudes. We must reach out across the divisions in our church, and find words that name a home big enough for us all.

Finally, we remember the cup which is poured out for many. We need to reach out for the fullness of the Kingdom. And this is hard in a society whose language is often marked by a flat literalism. We need the poets, the imagination of the young and off-beat, to open our hearts to the unsayable.

So we can see a rhythm here. Jesus reaches out to the silence of the disciples, and gathers them into his community, and then reaches out to the Kingdom. This is like the tempo of breathing, the filling and emptying of lungs. The vital moments of our history are always moments of humanity's lungs. God breathes into the lungs of Adam at the beginning, then Christ breathes out his last breath at the climax of salvation, and then the Holy Spirit is breathed upon us at Pentecost. Our preaching will be powerful if it lives by the rhythm of this breathing, humanity's own breathing giving oxygen to our blood, and God's deep breathing within us. Clement of Alexandria wrote, 'Breathing together is properly said of the church. For the sacrifice of the church is the word breathing as incense from holy souls, the sacrifice and the whole mind being at the same time unveiled in God.'[15]

Notice finally that this dramatic event of the Last Supper moves us from the silence of incomprehension to the silence of the mystery, from an empty silence to a plenary silence. We go from the silence of the disciples who understand nothing, to the silence of those who cannot find words for what they have glimpsed. The preacher lives within that space, begging for words. It is the gift of God's grace, what the early Dominicans called the *gratia praedicationis*, that propels us from the silence of poverty to the silence that is full.

---

15. *Stromata* VII. 6, in *Ante-Nicene Fathers II* 526f, quoted by Paul Janowiak *The Holy Preaching: the Sacramentality of the Word in the Liturgical Assembly* (Collegeville: Liturgical Press, 2000), 15.

Contributors

Bruce Barber

Bruce Barber is a Minister in the Uniting Church in Australia and was until recently the Dean of the United Faculty of Theology, Melbourne. He has taught Systematic Theology and Preaching in the United Faculty of Theology in Melbourne.

Vivian Boland OP

Vivian Boland is an Irish Dominican who lectures in theology at St Mary's University College, Twickenham as well as at Blackfriars, Oxford where he is Master of Students in the English Dominican Province. He recently published a major study of the thought of Thomas Aquinas from the point of view of his understanding of teaching and learning (*St Thomas Aquinas,* Continuum Library of Educational Thought Volume 1, (London and New York: Continuum, 2007).

Elaine Farmer

Elaine Farmer is an Anglican priest with a specialized ministry in preaching, both in Australia and internationally. She has taught homiletics at the Charles Sturt University School of Theology in Canberra and is also a writer and conference speaker.

Anthony Gooley

Anthony Gooley is a deacon of the Roman Catholic Archdiocese of Brisbane. He is working on his PhD in systematic theology through Griffith University/Brisbane College of Theology. He is investigating the place of a universal ministry of unity in Roman Catholic and

Orthodox dialogue within an ecclesiology of communion. He is a member of the Commission for Ecumenism and Interfaith Relations of Brisbane Archdiocese

Thorwald Lorenzen
For more than twenty years, Thorwald Lorenzen was Professor for Systematic Theology and Social Ethics at the International Baptist Theological Seminary in Rüschlikon, Switzerland. During the past ten years (19952005) he has served as the Senior Minister of the Canberra Baptist Church. In his official retirement from professional life, he is Professor of Theology and Principal Researcher at Charles Sturt University. He also lectures at St Mark's Theological Centre in Canberra and at Whitley College, University of Melbourne.

Timothy Radcliffe OP
Timothy Radcliffe was Master of the Dominicans (the Order of Preachers) between 1992 and 2001. At present he lives in Oxford and travels extensively, teaching and preaching for a variety of groups. He is the author of a number of acclaimed books that have been translated into many languages. His most recent book, *What is the Point of Being a Christian?* (London and New York: Continuum, 2005) was awarded the 2006 Michael Ramsey Prize for Theological Writing.

Romanos Stergiou
Romanos Stergiou is a graduate of St Andrew's Theological College, Sydney, a priest in the Greek Orthodox Archdiocese of Australia, and is working in the Parish of St Anna Parish, Gold Coast, Queensland.